WILLIAM MORRIS

WILLIAM MORRIS

the man and the myth

INCLUDING LETTERS OF
WILLIAM MORRIS
TO J. L. MAHON AND
DR. JOHN GLASSE

by
R. PAGE ARNOT

GREENWOOD PRESS, PUBLISHERS
WESTPORT, CONNECTICUT

Library of Congress Cataloging in Publication Data

Arnot, Robert Page, 1890-
  William Morris, the man and the myth.

    Reprint of the ed. published by Monthly Review Press,
New York.
    Includes bibliographical references and index.
    1. Morris, William, 1834-1896. 2. Mahon, John
Lincoln. 3. Glasse, John. 4. Socialists--Great
Britain. I. Morris, William, 1834-1896. II. Mahon,
John Lincoln. III. Glasse, John. IV. Title.
[HX243.A8 1976]   335'.0092'4   76-107
ISBN 0-8371-8652-8

First published in the United States in 1964 by Monthly
Review Press, New York

Reprinted with the permission of Monthly Review Press

Reprinted in 1976 by Greenwood Press,
a division of Williamhouse-Regency Inc.

Library of Congress Catalog Card Number 76-107

ISBN 0-8371-8652-8

Printed in the United States of America

CONTENTS

PREFACE

Bernard Shaw wrote of Morris some thirty years ago that "he towers greater and greater above the horizon beneath which his best-advertised contemporaries have disappeared". And that is still true today.

This book owes its appearance to several factors. The first is the finding in the latter part of 1962 of long-lost holograph letters of William Morris to John Lincoln Mahon, who was the first secretary of the Socialist League, founded 30th December, 1884.

The second is the opportunity thus afforded to have within the covers of a book the letters of Morris to Dr. Glasse, which received magazine publication (together with a handsome offprint) a dozen years ago.

Third, is the further opportunity to respond to insistent requests for a reprint of a booklet written by me many years ago. A reissue of this (*William Morris: a Vindication*) was out of the question: old polemics reprinted taste like a rehash: it would only have been "cauld kale het again". On the other hand it was necessary to furnish full explanation of each of the letters: and, more than this, to give the background without which it is hard to understand how the great poet and artist and master of design came to call himself a communist in the last twelve years of his life.

I have therefore cast the book in the form of six chapters, embodying in two chapters the newly discovered thirty letters of William Morris as well as the twenty made available at the beginning of the 'fifties shortly after the first extensive publication of the poet's intimate (family and friends) correspondence. These two chapters, together with passages cited from published works, make up nearly three-quarters of the book.

The first three chapters are introductory, clearing the

7

ground from accumulated myths and giving also something of the necessary background. In these, as also in the sixth chapter, I have made some considerable use of my old pamphlet: but, of course, much has to be said now that is new: and I have had to take account of the dozen or so excellent publications over the last thirty years. I acknowledge my debt to these good publications amid so much inferior stuff by listing them at the end of the sixth chapter.

The Mahon documents number thirty in all (twenty-nine letters and one resolution) of which twenty-eight are letters from Morris. Of these all with the exception of one headed with the firm's notepaper seem to have been written from Kelmscott House, Upper Mall, Hammersmith. They run from March, 1884, to April, 1888. Beyond the day and month Morris, like so many others, never added the year. In most cases internal evidence would have eased matters for a date-diviner. But this was rendered largely unnecessary by the fact that J. L. Mahon had kept the letters carefully and had added the date. Consequently there were only three letters in which there could be any dispute as to their location in time.

I have to thank his son, John A. Mahon, for making available in print these letters which bring up vividly the clash of personalities as well as policies in the 'eighties, the season of the revival of socialism in Great Britain.

The letters to John Glasse, twenty-one in number (including three postcards), run from February, 1886, to March, 1895. For the most part they are concerned with arrangements for lectures and journeys in Scotland, but amongst them over a dozen contain statements of the poet's outlook as well as details about the progress of his gospel, or, sometimes, about the obstacles and hazards. Finally, my thanks are due to *Labour Monthly*, in which two-thirds of these letters originally appeared and to Freeman Bass (honorary treasurer of the William Morris Society) through whose kindness they were made available for publication.

R.P.A.

24th March, 1964

CHAPTER ONE

THE MORRIS MYTH

WILLIAM MORRIS, artist, craftsman and poet, was born on 24th March, 1834, at Walthamstow in Essex, "a suburban village on the edge of Epping Forest". He was thus a Londoner like Geoffrey Chaucer and John Milton, even a suburbanite like John Keats. Morris came of a well-to-do bourgeois family,[1] and went through the routine of his class at public school and Oxford University. He wrote poems, was apprenticed to an architect, became a master craftsman in one field after another, from furniture designing to printing; became a manufacturer; took an active part in an anti-war association in the 'seventies; joined in 1883 a socialist organisation, agitated and organised; edited *The Commonweal*, to which Frederick Engels and Eleanor Marx contributed; and, after a life of intense and ceaseless activity over many fields, died at the age of sixty-two having remained to the end a revolutionary socialist.

William Morris, pretty well known in Europe in his lifetime, is still a name in the British Labour movement, while his fame has spread far beyond the English-speaking countries. His chants for socialists are heard at May Day demonstrations. His memory was revered by those who could recall him, especially his plain, simple habit of speech, essence of straightforwardness and revolutionary vigour. His writings on art and socialism still have an influence, and would have more but for the veil that has been cast around him. For, more than any other socialist leader of the nineteenth century, Morris has

1. In his fiftieth year William Morris wrote in reply to an inquiry: "We lived in the ordinary bourgeois style of comfort; and since we belonged to the evangelical section of the English Church I was brought up in what I should call rich establishmentarian puritanism; a religion which even as a boy I never took to."

been subjected to that "canonisation" of which Lenin set forth the stigmata:

During the lifetime of great revolutionaries, the oppressing classes have invariably meted out to them relentless persecution and received their teaching with the most savage hostility, most furious hatred and a ruthless campaign of slanders. After their death, however, attempts are usually made to turn them into harmless saints, canonising them, as it were, and investing their name with a certain halo, by way of "consolation" to the oppressed classes, and with the object of duping them, while at the same time emasculating and vulgarising the real essence of their revolutionary theories and blunting their revolutionary edge.

This halo-casting process set in early with William Morris, grew with each year after his death, until it reached a climax in the hundredth year after his birth. Then, in March, 1934, these words of Lenin were proven to apply faithfully. For this Englishman's centenary celebrations were turned into an orgy of "canonisation"; books poured forth "in his honour"; newspaper articles were written in dozens; and this "great Victorian" (did they ever read what Morris wrote of Queen Victoria?) was hoisted up to his niche as a "harmless saint". Thereafter this false effigy was set up as an object of worship.

Consequently this graven image of Morris has to be shattered before any estimate of him is possible. The myths built up about him have to be destroyed. There are at least two kinds of myth about William Morris. One, clearly "establishmentarian", is indeed the bourgeois myth: the other I may call the Menshevik myth, not simply as a handy alliterative code name for it but chiefly because it is lodged amongst European parties still belonging to that category of sixty years ago and still seeing history only from behind.

Thirty years ago the bourgeois myth, germinating from the first hints in Mackail's biography of 1899, was proclaimed to the world by a notable figure of the establishment. Stanley Baldwin, the iron-master who led the Conservative Party for fifteen years (and was thrice Prime Minister) till the 1937 Coronation finished his task, was chosen to open the great

1934 centenary exhibition at the Victoria and Albert Museum in South Kensington. In Baldwin's speech, and in newspaper comments upon it, there was no mention whatever of Morris as a revolutionary. He is a great poet, a great craftsman, a great artist, a great influence, a great what-not; but he is not mentioned as a revolutionary. Prime Ministers were not always as impudent as this. They gave the subject a wide berth. Some years earlier, when a predecessor of Baldwin as Prime Minister, the Earl of Oxford and Asquith, delivered his Romanes Lectures at Oxford on the "Great Victorians" he significantly omitted William Morris from the list. But by the 'thirties the Tory leader of the House of Commons— representative of the capitalist class, of "these foul swine" as they are called in *A Dream of John Ball*—had the impudence to scatter his mendacities over the memory of the man who said of the Parliament of his day that it was:

> on the one side a kind of watch committee, sitting to see that the interests of the upper classes took no hurt; and on the other hand a sort of blind to delude people into supposing that they had some share in the management of their own affairs.

Of course Morris was a great artist and a great craftsman; but neither his art nor his craftsman's work can be truly understood, nor can the whole man be understood, unless he is seen as he really was, as a revolutionary socialist, fighting for the overthrow of capitalism and for the victory of the working class.

The Menshevik myth, widely diffused in Britain and still more widely abroad, has always been of a different character. The picture is of Morris as "a gentle socialist" and fits in well with what Ramsay MacDonald, for many years leader of the British Labour Party before he ended as Prime Minister of a coalition (but predominantly Tory) government, once said of socialism—*his* socialism—that it was based not upon economics but had an historical, ethical "and literary" basis. William Morris was hardly dead before this myth began to be built up by Bruce Glasier and many others. The hash of "Appreciations" written for the Walthamstow Centenary Celebrations in several cases carried the myth into wildest travesty.[1] The burden of this Menshevik myth, as it has lingered on for over sixty years, is that Morris was "not a Marxist", and if there is now some assimilation of Morris and Marx in their scribblings it is only because they have at length created a mythical Marx to fit in with their mythical Morris. It does not matter to myth-mongers that Morris's first political utterances display his consciousness of class antagonism and class hatred; that these writings, beginning with the influence of John Ruskin, became more and more filled with the influence of Marx; that he joined a Marxist body; that, like Marx and Engels, he distrusted and broke with the founder of that first organisation; that, along with Marx's daughter, Eleanor, and other close associates, he founded and led a second Marxist organisation; that, on its behalf, he sponsored an international socialist Congress in Paris in 1889; and that in his whole writings during the period of his political activity Morris is accepting and following as best he can the teachings of Marx on political economy, the antagonism of classes in history and the strategy of the long struggle that would lead to a social revolution.

It should be realised that there is no question at all of these people weighing up the mistakes of Morris, as Frederick Engels did, estimating his serious errors in tactics. No. They simply brush aside the Morris that was, and construct a Morris that never existed, a sort of sickly dilettante socialist, as personally incredible as he would be politically monstrous.

What was the cause of this myth-building? The early myth-mongers, all of them bitterly anti-Marxist, found it intolerable that an artist whom some of them regarded as a new Michelangelo or a new Leonardo da Vinci should be counted a follower of Marx. So that in essence the fight over the body of Morris was a fight against the influence of Marx inside the Labour movement; and unfortunately the only socialist body based on the class struggle was dominated by leaders whose factional antagonism to Morris made them

1. "He was a great Distributist", wrote G. K. Chesterton.

willing to leave his reputation in the hands of the traducers without a protest.

The result was that in the first decades of this century old associates of William Morris could be found who would calmly state that he had not even studied Marx. What evidence was brought forward for this? Can it be believed that the only substantial evidence is a statement in his article for *Justice* of 16th June, 1894, in the series "How I became a Socialist"?

> Whereas I thoroughly enjoyed the historical part of *Capital*, I suffered agonies of confusion of the brain over reading the pure economics of that great work.

Everyone knows that the first chapters of *Capital* are difficult: as much is stated by Marx himself as well as by Engels (and also by Lenin), and the only meaning of this sentence is that Morris was honest enough to confess his difficulties. Yet, actually, the meaning of this sentence was somehow twisted to make the proof that Morris was an anti-Marxist. Starting from the axiom "Morris not a Marxist", they then proceed on the evidence of ill-remembered gossip to rule out all in his writings that is evidence to the contrary.

It will be necessary in the course of this book to deal with various examples of this distortion of Morris's actual words. Meantime, a few brief references will serve to smash their axiom, "Morris not a Marxist".

First, in *A Summary of the Principles of Socialism*, written by H. M. Hyndman and William Morris and published in 1883 by the newly founded Democratic Federation, the standpoint taken, whatever its imperfections, is most distinctly intended to be Marxist.

Secondly, in the short and telling *Manifesto of the Socialist League* (December, 1884), written solely by Morris, the thought, expressed with great simplicity, is even more explicitly Marxist.

Thirdly, in the papers of J. L. Mahon, first Secretary of the Socialist League, there is a single handwritten sheet, ascribed to Morris in the following words: "M.S.S. by

W. Morris. Found in his copy of *Capital* which he gave me about 1888–1890. (signed) J. L. Mahon 8/2/24." It is a summary of one of the portions of "pure economics" and is to be found in the twenty-fifth chapter of "this great work".

Lastly, in *The Commonweal* series, called "Socialism from the Root Up"[1] (1886–7), jointly written by William Morris and Belfort Bax, an attempt is made to trace the development of society from earliest times in the light of historical materialism. Chapters of particular interest are those in which Utopian Socialism is analysed and condemned (and yet in the Morris-myth Morris is referred to as a Utopian Socialist!) and that other entitled "Scientific Socialism: Karl Marx", in which the argument of *Capital* is summarised and defended. This last book proved a snag for the myth-mongers; amongst them Bruce Glasier (editor for many years of *The Labour Leader*) who wrote memoirs on Morris published in 1921. Glasier, who was busy re-making Morris in his own image (see the ridiculous chapter on "Morris and Religion", where Glasier, himself deep in the swamp of religiosity, flounders pitifully around Morris's explicit statement: "I am what is called bluntly an atheist"), had the effrontery to suggest that *Socialism: Its Growth and Outcome* represented the views of Bax but not those of Morris, who "belonged to the old Utopian school rather than to the modern Scientific Socialist School of thought". The answer to this slander by Glasier had already been given by Morris and Bax in their preface, in which they wrote:

> We have only further to add that the work has been in the true sense of the word a *collaboration*, each sentence having been carefully considered by both the authors in common, although now one, now the other, has had more to do with the initial suggestions in different portions of the work.

But it was clearly necessary for the myth-mongers that the chapters of that book, with their fully Marxist outlook, had to be discounted at all costs.

1. Afterwards republished in book form under the title of *Socialism: Its Growth and Outcome* (1893).

14

CHAPTER TWO

GROWTH OF A REVOLUTIONARY

How did Morris come to be a revolutionary socialist, and how did he come to join a Marxist organisation?

The usual explanation is to treat of Morris's "excursion into socialism" as some sort of aberration of the poet, one of those things which show what fantastic fellows artists are. When this usual explanation is furbished forth in its right-wing Labour variety (the Menshevik myth) it is the revolutionary character of his socialism that is regarded as the aberration. This essentially philistine view of the development of any great artist or fighter is buttressed up by sentimental reflections on struggles that Morris had to carry through inside the socialist body to which he belonged—all written in the offensive kindly manner of a doctor descanting on an imbecile patient—and on the other hand by sham versions of the history of the 'eighties and the three preceding decades.

Actually the clue to the development of Morris is relatively simple and obvious. Morris left Oxford a rebel against capitalism, without, however, knowing capitalism and its meaning and its cause except as a manifestation of ugliness, anarchy and bad conditions for the mass of the people. Wholly unacquainted at that point with the life of the working class, and unaware of the existence of the Marxian socialism—this was in the later 'fifties—he was nevertheless aware of the writings of Carlyle and his school, of the feudal socialists. Thomas Carlyle, in his *Past and Present*, as well as in his *Latter-day Pamphlets* and *Chartism*, had adopted a standpoint which could be classed as feudal socialism, and—though this twenty years afterwards rattled down to a support of slavery—Carlyle's earlier eloquent comparison of the lot of a wage-worker amid the Chartist struggles with the lot of a serf seven hundred years before was sufficiently striking to draw commendation from Engels at the time. Morris was affected by this school, and it is to be noted that there is a certain resemblance between Morris's treatment of the Middle Ages and what Engels discerned in the germ in Carlyle as "a curious apotheosis of medieval times".

Linked, too, with feudal socialism, as is pointed out in the *Communist Manifesto* of 1848, was Christian Socialism, which, under Frederick Dennison Maurice, Charles Kingsley and others, was flourishing in the 'fifties. John Ruskin, who was to horrify the vulgar economists by his *Unto This Last*, was also writing; and his books, as Morris recollected, "were at the time a sort of revelation to me". The Working Men's College in Crowndale Road, London, had taken John Ruskin and Dante Gabriel Rossetti as its art teachers. But the voice of the Chartists was muted, and it was at first to the influence of these other kinds of socialism that Morris was subjected.

In the circumstances it is not surprising that the gifted young artist, with powers yet unexplored, should from the very beginning show a fierce hatred of capitalism. At first the expression of this attitude to capitalism takes variant forms: it takes the form of delight in other periods of history that were brought to him in his childhood, first by Walter Scott, whose Waverley novels young William had read by the time he was seven, and then by all the minsters seen and the books read in his youth, culminating in *The Canterbury Tales* of "My Master, GEOFFREY CHAUCER". It is shown also in his attempt to change the expression of civilisation in its arts; in his hatred of the conventions of bourgeois society, its customs, its costumes, its furniture, its decorations and patterns, its cant and hypocrisy. Not until twenty years have passed does this hatred of capitalism begin to take on a political form. But it endures all the time, increases, deepens and grows to be a fiery, unquenchable fury against capitalism, "a lightning flame, a shearing sword, a storm to overthrow".

Meantime, in his poetry—*The Defence of Guenevere* (1858), *The Life and Death of Jason* (1867), *The Earthly Paradise* (1868–70), *Love is Enough* (1872)—Morris re-tells the stories of

16

other times, and re-creates the world that is gone. Not once does he deal with the capitalist centuries. These poems, expressing in this negative way his attitude to capitalism, are also to some extent an escape from it. Later, when he comes to grips with capitalism, the poet becomes merged in the revolutionary fighter.

Throughout all this period Morris regards with eyes of hatred the "art products" of capitalism. He sees the worker made into a cog in the machine, while he does not (as some of his philistine critics seem to imagine) teach a hatred of machines. But he does intuitively grasp the fact which Marx was to express in classic form in *Capital* that:

Within the capitalist system all methods for raising the social productiveness of labour are brought about at the cost of the individual labourer; all means for the development of production transform themselves into means of domination over, and exploitation of, the producers; they mutilate the labourer into a fragment of a man, degrade him to the level of an appendage of a machine, destroy every remnant of charm in his work and turn it into a hated toil; they estrange him from the intellectual potentialities of the labour-process in the same proportion as science is incorporated in it as an independent power; they distort the conditions under which he works, subject him during the labour process to a despotism the more hateful for its meanness; they transform his life-time into working-time and drag his wife and child beneath the wheels of the Juggernaut of Capital.

How true this is can be judged from something published a hundred years after Morris's birth in a worker's answer to a motor manufacturer. The motor magnate, standing at the microphone dully repeating the Whig panegyrics of machinery, had said:

Mechanisation is now relieving the brain of the old tediums and giving it a new stimulus . . . slaves of to-day being made of metal, while the mind of man directs.

To this twaddle there was given a terrible answer from William Ferrie, a motor mechanic, whose statement (duly banned by the British Broadcasting Corporation) might well be an additional footnote to Part IV of *Capital*:

> I'd like [he said] to take you on a trip through a modern motor plant, then you'd be able to see for yourselves whether the slaves are made of metal or not . . . In the old days the trimming or upholstering of a car was done by a group of four trimmers. They did the complete job: ordering, measuring, cutting, matching, fitting, fixing, and finishing. They were craftsmen. The finished production was the work of this small group, and I am sure there was pride in their eyes as they walked around the finished cabriolet.
> Nowadays what do you see? In the trim shop of the modern factory the conveyor belt has been put in. Hundreds of men carry out small jobs—some of them taking only a few minutes. Everyone is working against the clock. . . .
> When I hear it said that man is master of the machine, and that the slaves of the day are made of metal, I can't help smiling rather cynically. I'll tell you this: the machine enslaves us. It compels us to do its bidding. We have to accept its pace and follow its commands. The conveyor belt is our master. If the management in the factory decide to increase speed by ten per cent, a thousand hands work ten per cent faster. I am not exaggerating when I say that those of us who work on the conveyor belt are bound to it as galley slaves were bound to the galley. [5th March, 1934]

Morris, with his grasp of the results of the application of machinery by the capitalist method of production, concentrated his attention first on the products of this industry and especially on the consumer-wares of the mid-nineteenth century. He looked on it all and saw that it was ugly: and he pierced through to the root cause in the division of labour and the toilsome life of the exploited worker. While he witnessed this mortal disease of the domestic arts, so that ugliness reigned along with Queen Victoria in Buckingham Palace and in Balmoral, which she and her Prince Consort had spattered indiscriminately with tartan wallpapers, as well as in the tenements and hovels of the mass of the people, he saw on the other hand that art in its process of perishing had reached the stage of becoming the preserve of a small section of the upper classes. All that art had meant in the life of mankind had become narrowed down to fine arts for fine ladies and fine gentlemen. Morris detested this anaemia of the arts, just as he detested the flat ugliness of the ordinary consumption products of capitalism. So Morris reached the two-fold conclusion: first, that art must perish unless it be a people's art; secondly, that the worker must be an artist and the artist must be a worker. For art, he said, is the result of man's joy in his labour. It was to the working out of the second conclusion that Morris first applied himself. Rich enough to have a house built according to his fancy and to be decorated by his pre-Raphaelite friends, he found that there was no furniture in the market that he could tolerate in his house. There were neither beds to lie in nor chairs to sit upon, neither tables, nor carpets, curtains, hangings, tableware or any other furnishing. Oxford Street and Tottenham Court Road and all the other shopping centres in every town in England were one Sahara of ugliness, both costly ugliness and ugliness that was cheap and nasty.

Therefore he set himself to be the maker of goods that could be produced by worker-artists, that would serve their use, be a pleasure to the eye, a joy to the maker and the user. A firm of himself and his friends was established, and presently Morris was turning out furniture, upholstery and all kinds of decorative ware. Later it was to be carpets; the revival of the art of weaving; the revival of the use of the old vegetable dyes, which gave brighter and better colours than the aniline dye then in its crudest stage; the revival of high-warp tapestry, in which he made pictures the like of which had never been seen before; and, finally, the revival of the art of printing. Each of these was taken up, one after the other, and all of them continued to the end of his life of ceaseless activity.

All of these changes made by Morris could only be fully developed and used in a different kind of society. Morris became more and more aware of this, more and more certain that all his ordinary capacities as a craftsman must be thwarted, narrowed and confined, so long as capitalism existed; and not only his own capacities but the million-fold potentialities of all other workers; while even what little could be done by him, or by all other artists, could not be appreciated by the masses of mankind in their life of toil and penury. In *The Pilgrims of Hope* he asks:

> The poets have sung and the builders have
> builded,
> The painters have fashioned their tales of
> delight;
> For what and for whom has the world's book
> been gilded,
> When all is for these but the blackness of
> night?

Thus Morris became increasingly conscious of the contradictions of capitalism, appearing to him first in their effect on the art superstructure of society. This consciousness finds expression, and extremely poignantly, in one place: in the preface to *The Earthly Paradise*, where he writes:

> Dreamer of dreams, born out of my due time,
> Why should I strive to set the crooked straight?
> Let it suffice me that my murmuring rhyme
> Beats with light wing against the ivory gate,
> Telling a tale not too importunate
> To those who in the sleepy region stay,
> Lulled by the singer of an empty day.
>
> Folk say a wizard to a northern king
> At Christmas-tide such wondrous things did show,
> That through one window men beheld the spring,
> And through another saw the summer glow,
> And through a third the fruited vines a-row,
> While still, unheard, but in its wonted way,
> Piped the drear wind of that December day.
>
> So with this Earthly Paradise it is,
> If ye will read aright, and pardon me,
> Who strive to build a shadowy isle of bliss
> Midmost the beating of the steely sea,
> Where tossed about all hearts of men must be;
> Whose ravening monsters mighty men shall slay,
> Not the poor singer of an empty day.

The meaning is unmistakable: Morris sees the problem though he does not yet see how he can solve it. Merely this insight raises him above the ranks of contemporary artists and poets; a higher stage still is to be reached, when the gifted artist, poet and craftsman, hater of capitalism, casts by his hesitation and sets out himself to slay the ravening monsters, leaving behind him for ever "the poor singer of an empty day".

The ascent into politics was preceded by the decade of the 'seventies, wherein Morris found inspiration for struggle, on the one hand in the Icelandic sagas, and on the other hand in an anti-war agitation led by him. The extraordinarily potent effect upon Morris of the Icelandic Middle Ages, a society of quite a different type from European feudalism, requires more than passing mention. Here was a society with class antagonisms little developed, as is shown by the very rudi-mentary form of the state power, but where, on the other hand, the struggle of man with nature came to the forefront. The history of the struggles between Viking families and their descendants against this background of the struggle of man with nature, grim, harsh and terrifying, forms the content of the Icelandic sagas. Just as medieval Iceland differed in its class structure from medieval Europe, so too its literature. The difference can be most clearly brought out in the attitude to the supernatural. The supernatural exists in the Icelandic sagas, but there is no such helplessness and craven yielding as characterised much of medieval literature, product of material and spiritual exploitation of serfs. If there were no snakes in Iceland there were no monks either. The parasitic classes typical of feudal times are not to be found in the sagas. The supernatural is met with, and fought with and overcome. Grettir, in the saga, goes out and grapples to the death with the murderous ghost of Glam the Thrall.

Morris was powerfully affected by this literature, in which the quality of courage is so highly developed as to make much of contemporary medieval literature appear like bravado. He helped to translate many of the sagas and twice, in 1871 and 1873, he made what was then the unusual journey to

21

Iceland, where he trod the wastes and deserts hallowed for him by the saga heroes. The culmination of his Icelandic studies was that he translated the *Volsunga Saga* (1870), the epic story that was to the other sagas (especially in its verse form in the *Elder Edda*) what Homer had been to the classic literature of Greece. As he himself says:

> For this is the great story of the North, which should be to all our race what the Tale of Troy was to the Greeks— to all our race first, and afterwards, when the change of the world has made our race nothing more than a name of what has been, a story too—then should it be to those that come after us no less than the Tale of Troy has been to us.

This story was afterwards re-cast by him in English verse in *Sigurd the Volsung and the Fall of the Niblungs* (1877), the greatest epic poem of the nineteenth century. The towering courage and spirit of the epic is unmistakable, and tells us something of what its writer was becoming.[1] Iceland of the sagas had nerved Morris for the epic struggle of the classes in Britain.

The first skirmishes of Morris's entry into public agitation were also in 1877. In March of that year he wrote to the *Athenaeum* in protest against the destruction of so many cathedrals and parish churches by the architect Sir Gilbert Scott and others—"acts of barbarism which the modern architect, parson and squire call 'restoration' "—and urged the setting up of an association for "protecting these relics". The wording of this appeal (from which resulted the Society for the Protection of Ancient Buildings) was uncompromising: "I admit", wrote the poet, "that the architects are, with very

1. Seven years later Engels in a letter to Marx's daughter, Laura Lafargue, tells of an "Art Evening" of the socialists on 21st November, 1884, in Bloomsbury ("I did not go, as I do not as yet see my way to sitting three hours consecutively in a stiff chair") and adds: "Bax played the piano—rather long—Morris who was here the other night and quite delighted to find the Old Norse Edda on my table—he is an Icelandic enthusiast—Morris read a piece of his poetry . . . (the description of Brynhild burning herself with Sigurd's corpse), etc., etc., it went off very well —their art seems to be rather better than their literature and their poetry better than their prose." The first item of that evening was a pianoforte duet by Kathleen Ina and G. Bernard Shaw.

few exceptions, hopeless, because interest, habit and ignorance bind them, and that the clergy are hopeless, because their order, habit and an ignorance yet grosser, bind them."

Morris was still more deeply stirred that spring of 1877 by the war-danger that had arisen and, as he told some six years later, "I also thoroughly dreaded the outburst of Chauvinism which swept over the country", particularly because of its effect on "social questions". He goes on: "I therefore took an active part in the anti-Turk agitation, was a member of the committee of the Eastern Question Association and worked hard at it." How far by this time he had progressed from "the idle singer of an empty day" is clear from his *Unjust War*, a personal manifesto, significantly addressed "To the working-men of England".[1] The writer, though still a member of the Liberal Party, is already putting on his armour for the class struggle. That arming was to be completed in the ranks of a socialist organisation, in the inspiration of the example of the Communards of Paris, the first fighters for the dictatorship of the proletariat, and in the study of the teachings of Karl Marx.

Morris did not become a literary socialist or an artistic socialist, or any other kind of middle-class parody of a socialist. Morris became a revolutionary socialist. When he declared himself to be a socialist, or, as he once said, became "one of the Communist folk", it was precisely in the meaning of the last words of the *Communist Manifesto*, written by Marx and Engels thirty-five years before:

> The Communists disdain to conceal their views and aims. They openly declare that their ends can be attained only by the forcible overthrow of all existing social conditions. Let the ruling classes tremble at a Communist revolution. In it the proletarians have nothing to lose but their chains. They have a world to win.
>
> WORKING MEN OF ALL COUNTRIES, UNITE!

1. Reproduced at the end of this chapter.

UNJUST WAR

To the Working-men of England

Friends and fellow-citizens,

There is danger of war; bestir yourselves to face that danger: if you go to sleep, saying we do not understand it, and the danger is far off, you may wake and find the evil fallen upon you, for even now it is at the door. Take heed in time and consider it well, for a hard matter it will be for most of us to bear war-taxes, war-prices, war-losses of wealth and work and friends and kindred: we shall pay heavily, and you, friends of the working classes, will pay the heaviest.

And what shall we buy at this heavy price? Will it be glory, and wealth and peace for those that come after us? Alas! no; for these are the gains of a *just* war; but if we wage the *unjust* war that fools and cowards are bidding us wage to-day, our loss of wealth will buy us fresh losses of wealth, our loss of work will buy us loss of hope, our loss of friends and kindred will buy us enemies from father to son.

An unjust war, I say: for do not be deceived! if we go to war with Russia now, it will not be to punish her for evil deeds done, or to hinder her from evil deeds hereafter, but to put down just insurrection against the thieves and murderers of Turkey; to stir up a faint pleasure in the hearts of the do-nothing fools that cry out without meaning for a "spirited foreign policy"; to guard our well-beloved rule in India from the coward fear of an invasion that may happen a hundred years hence—or never; to exhibit our army and navy once more before the wondering eyes of Europe; to give a little hope to our holders of Turkish bonds: Working-men of England, which of these things do you think worth starving for, worth dying for? Do all of them rolled into one make that body of *English Interests* we have heard of lately?

24

And who are they who flaunt in our faces the banner
inscribed on one side *English Interests*, and on the other
Russian Misdeeds? Who are they that are leading us into
war? Let us look at these saviours of England's honour, these
champions of Poland, these scourges of Russia's iniquities!
Do you know them? Greedy gamblers on the Stock Exchange,
idle officers of the army and navy (poor fellows!), worn-out
mockers of the Clubs, desperate purveyors of exciting war-
news for the comfortable breakfast tables of those who
have nothing to lose by war, and lastly, in the place of
honour, the Tory Rump, that we fools, weary of peace,
reason and justice, chose at the last election to "represent"
us: and over all their captain, the ancient place-hunter,
who, having at last climbed into an Earl's chair, grins
down thence into the anxious face of England, while his
empty heart and shifty head is compassing the stroke that will
bring on our destruction perhaps, our confusion certainly:
O shame and double shame, if we march under such a
leadership as this in an unjust war against a people who are
not our enemies, against Europe, against freedom, against
nature, against the hope of the world.

Working-men of England, one word of warning yet:
I doubt if you know the bitterness of hatred against freedom
and progress that lies at the hearts of a certain part of the
richer classes in this country: their newspapers veil it in a
kind of decent language; but do but hear them talking
among themselves, as I have often, and I know not whether
scorn or anger would prevail in you at their folly and
insolence: these men cannot speak of your order, of its aims,
of its leaders without a sneer or an insult: these men, if they
had the power (may England perish rather), would thwart
your just aspirations, would silence you, would deliver
you bound hand and foot for ever to irresponsible capital
—and these men, I say it deliberately, are the heart and
soul of the party that is driving us to an unjust war: can
the Russian people be your enemies or mine like these men
are, who are the enemies of all justice? They can harm us
but little now, but if war comes, *unjust war*, with all its
confusion and anger, who shall say what their power may be,
what step backward we may make? Fellow-citizens, look
to it, and if you have any wrongs to be redressed, if you
cherish your most worthy hope of raising your whole order

peacefully and solidly, if you thirst for leisure and knowledge, if you long to lessen those inequalities which have been our stumbling-block since the beginning of the world, then cast aside sloth and cry out against an UNJUST WAR, and urge us of the Middle Classes to do no less, so that we may all protest solemnly and perseveringly against our being dragged (and who knows for why?) into an UNJUST WAR, in which, if we are victorious, we shall win shame, loss and rebuke; and if we are overpowered—what then?

Working-men of England I do not believe that in the face of your strenuous opposition, the opposition of those men whom war most concerns, any English Government will be so mad as to trap England and Europe into an UNJUST WAR.

A Lover of Justice

11th May, 1877

26

THE SOCIALIST LEAGUE

SOMETIME in these first years of public agitation Morris became a convinced socialist—while as yet there was in Britain no declared socialist organisation. As soon as there was one, Morris was now sure to be in; for as early as August, 1881, he writes in a letter: "To do nothing but grumble and not to act—that is throwing away one's life." Two years later he writes to Andreas Scheu that "I always intended to join any body who distinctly called themselves socialists" and goes on to explain that when he had accepted an invitation in 1882 "to join the Democratic Federation" it was in the hope that "it would declare for socialism". The invitation had come from Henry Mayers Hyndman—who some thirty years later was described by Lenin as "an English bourgeois philistine, who, being of the best in his class, in the long run beats out the road to socialism for himself, never fully getting rid of bourgeois traditions, bourgeois views and prejudices". Hyndman began his plunge in the socialist direction badly, with a sort of plagiarism of Marx. Karl Marx in the last letter to his friend F. A. Sorge wrote:

In the beginning of June, there was published by a certain Hyndman (who had before intruded himself into my house) a little book: *England for All*. It pretends to be written as an *exposé* of the programme of the "Democratic Federation"— a recently formed association of different English and Scotch radical societies, half bourgeois, half proletaires. The chapters on Labour and Capital are only literal extracts from, or circumlocutions of, the *Capital*, but the fellow does neither quote the book, nor its author, but to shield himself from exposure remarks at the end of his preface: "For the ideas and much of the matter contained in Chapters II and III, I am indebted to the work of a great thinker and original writer, etc. etc." Vis-à-vis myself, the fellow wrote stupid letters of excuse, for instance, that "the English don't like to be taught by foreigners," that "my name was so much detested, etc." With all that, his little book—so far as it pilfers the *Capital*—makes good propaganda, although the man is a "weak" vessel, and very far from having even the patience—the first condition of learning anything—of studying a matter thoroughly. All those amiable middle-class writers—if not specialists— have an itching to make money or name or political capital *immediately* out of any new thoughts they may have got at by any favourable windfall. Many evenings this fellow has pilfered from me, in order—to take me out and to learn in the easiest way. [15th December, 1881]

What was the situation of the English working-class movement at the moment when this Democratic Federation (in 1883) proclaimed itself socialist? The answer to this question is to be found in the letters of Frederick Engels to August Bebel and other leaders of the German Social-Democratic Party:

> Do not on any account whatever let yourself be deluded into thinking there is a real proletarian movement going on here. I know Liebknecht tries to delude himself and all the world about this, but it is not the case. The elements at present active may become important since they have accepted our theoretical programme and so acquired a basis, but only if a spontaneous movement breaks out here among the workers and they succeed in getting control of it. Till then they will remain individual minds, with a hotch-potch of confused sects, remnants of the great movement of the 'forties, standing behind them and nothing more. And—apart from the unexpected—a really general workers' movement will only come into existence here when the workers are made to feel the fact that England's world monopoly is broken.
>
> Participation in the domination of the world market was and is the basis of the political nullity of the English workers. The tail of the bourgeoisie in the economic exploitation of this monopoly but nevertheless sharing in its advantages, politically they are naturally the tail of the "great Liberal Party". [30th August, 1883]

28

A satisfactory history of the 'eighties and 'nineties has still to be written. Here we are concerned only with the progress in socialism of Morris, who early in 1883 had got hold of Marx's *Capital* in the French translation and was reading it with the greatest assiduity and delight. From this moment onwards the teachings of Marx in *Capital* begin to shine through Morris's writings, letters and speeches. At first, indeed, like that earlier socialist manufacturer, Robert Owen, Morris hoped that "leaders of society", or, at any rate, that artistic section with which he was best acquainted, would be ready to join the ranks of the class struggle. So we find him writing to Algernon Swinburne and others, but without success. Presently, however, Morris, in writing to a friend who thought that change depended on "individuals of good will belonging to all classes", says outright:

The upper and middle classes as a body will by the very nature of their existence resist the abolition of classes. I have never underrated the power of the middle classes, whom, in spite of their individual good nature and banality, I look upon as a most terrible and implacable force.

To destroy this force by the power of the revolutionary workers consciously fighting for its overthrow had now become Morris's chief end in life. "The antagonism of classes, which the system has bred, is the natural and necessary instrument of its destruction" (letter to C. E. Maurice, 1st July, 1883).

In the Social-Democratic Federation Morris, rather against his own will—he had wanted to be a "rank-and-filer"—found himself playing a leading part: but a leading part in that little organisation meant either submission to its founder or opposition. That opposition, in which participated Eleanor Marx, Karl Marx's youngest daughter, her husband Edward Aveling, Belfort Bax, Frederick Lessner, J. L. Mahon, Andreas Scheu, as well as Morris, became more and more opposed to Hyndman's methods. At length, at the end of 1884, the leading group were driven by Hyndman's behaviour to force matters to an issue, and by a majority passed a vote of censure on him: and then, as a majority, withdrew from the organisation, the main reason being, as Engels said, "because the whole Federation was nothing but a swindle".

The seceders then formed the Socialist League on 30th December, 1884. Within two months they had brought out a new paper, the famous *Commonweal*. Engels, who had helped to organise the secession, was nevertheless not over-sanguine as to the prospects, as may be seen from his letter to Eduard Bernstein:

> Those who resigned [he wrote at the time] were Aveling, Bax and Morris, the only honest men among the intellectuals but were as unpractical (two poets and one philosopher) as you could possibly find. In addition, the better of the known workers. They want to act in the London branches; they hope to win the majority and then let Hyndman carry on with his non-existent provincial branches. Their organ will be a little monthly journal. Finally they will work on a modest scale, in proportion to their forces, and no longer act as though the English proletariat were bound to follow as soon as a few intellectuals became converted to socialism and sounded the call. Their entire strength in London was (on Morris's admission) less than four hundred: in the provinces they had not a hundred supporters. [29th December, 1884]

So that was how they began, "the feeble band, the few". But the quality of the new organisation, its fearless outlook at its first beginnings, was of a very high order. This quality can be far better shown by a single extensive quotation than by a series of shorter extracts: and for this purpose choice must fall upon a very early declaration against a colonial war of aggression. It may be taken as the first anti-imperialist manifesto of the socialist movement in Britain, written when the tide was setting in strongly for annexations and protectorates in Asia and Africa.

ON THE SUDAN WAR

(March 2nd, 1885)

Fellow Citizens:

A wicked and unjust war is now being waged by the ruling and propertied classes of this country, with all the

30

resources of civilisation at their back, against an ill-armed and semi-barbarous people whose only crime is that they have risen against a foreign oppression which those classes themselves admit to have been infamous. Tens of millions wrung from the labour of workmen of this country are being squandered on Arab slaughtering; and for what: (1) that Eastern Africa may be "opened up" to the purveyor of "shoddy" wares, bad spirits, venereal disease, cheap bibles and the missionary; in short, that the English trader and contractor may establish his dominion on the ruins of the old, simple and happy life led by the children of the desert; (2) that a fresh supply of sinecure Government posts may be obtained for the occupation of the younger sons of the official classes; (3) as a minor consideration may be added that a new and happy hunting ground be provided for military sportsmen, who, like the late-lamented Colonel Burnaby, find life boring at home and are always ready for a little Arab shooting when occasion arises. All these ends determine the dominant classes, though in different proportions, to the course they are pursuing.

Citizens, you are the dupes of a plot. Be not deceived by the flimsy pretences that have been, and are, alleged as reasons for the cowardly brigandage perpetrated on weak and uncivilised peoples by these classes in the name of the community. Rest assured the above are the sole motives animating them, whatever their professions; in brief, that, in the words of our manifesto, "all the rivalries of nations have been reduced to this one—a degrading struggle for their share of the spoils of barbarous countries to be used at home for the purpose of increasing the riches of the rich and the poverty of the poor".

With the history and causes of the bondholders' war in Egypt you are probably already sufficiently familiar, but we invite your attention for a moment to the leading facts in this latest development of a career of hypocrisy and crime. After the British conquest of Egypt, General Hicks is allowed to attempt the reconquest of the Sudan in the interest of Egyptian usury. This attempt failing, General Baker is authorised to subdue at least the seaboard. A second failure demonstrating the utter futility of Egyptian arms against the desert spearmen, a fluttering in the dovecotes of the military and the Stock Exchange worlds ensues.

But there is balm in Gilead yet. Happy thought, the garrisons—yes, they must be rescued! General Gordon, the successful subduer of rebels in China, and ex-Governor-General at Khartoum, is he not the man to deal with Sudanese malcontents? Assuredly, say the *Pall Mall Gazette* and *The Times*. Cabinet ministers, unable to resist the mandates of the classes these powerful organs represent, bow their heads and submit.

Gordon, after duly consulting with his friends, is despatched, bearing in his hands the instructions of the Government, but—as events have proved—in his *pocket* those of the distinguished newspapers in question. Arrived at Khartoum, the "Christian hero", accordingly with scarcely a feint at negotiation, and in defiance of his professions of peace, proceeds to fortify himself within the city, and use it as a base for military raids upon the surrounding tribes, who he had previously cajoled with protestations of friendship. The play after this move was easy. The wicked Mahdi menaces the life of the "hero"; "hero" demands an expedition to help him "smash the Mahdi". The "rebels", otherwise Sudanese, are base enough to take their own town of Berber from the Egyptian garrison. "Christian hero" feels it his bounden duty to announce his intention of recapturing Berber, and putting all its inhabitants to the sword by way of chastisement. (This pious intention, fortunately for the Berberese, remained unrealised.) Meanwhile, garrisons are forgotten. The Jingoes know a cry worth two of that. Gordon abandoned! Despatch your expedition! cry *The Times*, *Pall Mall Gazette*, and company. Cabinet ministers faintly remonstrate and at length again bow their heads. Who are ministers to dispute the orders of influential newspapers representing important interests?

> Theirs not to reason why,
> Theirs not to make reply;
> Theirs but to do and—die,

and dying they are, to all appearances, as Cabinet ministers —of *Pall Mall Gazette*. That, however, is no concern of ours.

The expedition is despatched. British cut-throats slaughter a few thousand Arabs amid the jubilation of the Press, when —oh horror!—Khartoum is fallen: and fallen, too, into the hands of the Sudanese themselves. Gordon, no more! In Fleet Street is there a cry heard; lamentation and weeping and great mourning. Never was the dust of a hero so watered by the gush of newspaper before. Nowadays, however, we produce emotion like other things—primarily for profit—and only secondarily for use. Time was when men poured forth each his own grief in his own manner when they sorrowed for some great departed. Under the rule of the great industry we have changed all this. Now the factory system and the division of labour superseded individual emotion: it is distilled for us by the journalist, and we buy it ready made from the great vats in Fleet Street and Printinghouse Square. The result is that the public sometimes have emotion forced upon them when it suits the purveyor, for other reasons than the greatness of the departed. Perhaps it is so in this case. Anyway, from the well-watered dust of Gordon rises up for *The Times Pall Mall* and their clients, the fair prospect of British Protectorate at Khartoum, railway from Suakim to Berber, new markets, fresh colonial posts, etc. Cabinet ministers once more bow before the all-powerful press, and whispering they will ne'er consent, consent—to the reconquest of the country in the interest of English commerce—for the permanent railway from Suakim to Berber can mean nothing less than this.

Citizens, if you have any sense of justice, any manliness left in you, join us in our protest against the wicked and infamous act of brigandage now being perpetrated for the interest solely of the "privileged" classes of this country; an act of brigandage led up to through the foulest stream of well planned hypocrisy and fraud that has ever disgraced the foreign policy, even of this commercial age. Mehemet Achmet (the Mahdi) the brave man who, in Oriental fashion, is undertaking the deliverance of his country, has repeatedly declared through his agents his willingness to release the Bashi-Bazouk garrison and give guarantees to refrain from aggression in Egypt. Mr. Wilfrid Scawen Blunt was in a position, even when the "Christian hero" was wantonly waging an offensive war against the Mahdi, to ensure the success of the negotiations for his release, as well as that of the garrisons, had he been allowed to make them, as he assuredly would, had this been the real object in view, but such an arrangement was not quite good enough for the market-hunters and filibusters for whom the "influential" press writes. "Not this man, but Wolseley", cried they; and Wolseley was sent, avowedly to rescue their nominee—who by that ostentatious pietism which, as they were well aware, gilds everything with a certain section of the British public, had already so well served their turn— but in reality to engage in the conquest of the devoted land upon which from the first their vultures' eyes had been cast.

And, finally, we ask you to consider who it is that have to do the fighting on this and similar occasions. Is it the market-hunting classes themselves? Is it they who form the rank and file of the army? No! but the sons and brothers of the working classes at home. They it is who for a miserable pittance are compelled to serve in these commercial wars. They it is who conquer for the wealthy, middle and upper classes, new lands for exploitation, fresh populations for pillage, as these classes require them, and who have, as their reward, the assurance of their masters that they are "nobly fighting for their Queen and country".

The Provisional Council of the Socialist League—

W. Bridges Adams	Frank Kitz
Edward Aveling	Joseph Lane
Eleanor Marx Aveling	Frederick Lessner
Robert Banner	Thomas Maguire (Leeds)
E. Belfort Bax	J. L. Mahon
Thomas Binning	S. Mainwaring
H. Charles	James Mavor (Glasgow)
William J. Clark	William Morris
J. Cooper	C. Mowbray
E. T. Craig	Andreas Scheu (Edinburgh)
C. J. Faulkner (Oxford)	Edward Watson
W. Hudson	

A couple of generations later Lytton Strachey acquired or at any rate enlarged his fame by the "debunking" of General Gordon, who had been furbished up as "a hero of the Empire" for use in schools. But the job had already been done, and on the spot, by William Morris, who at this time was responsible for drafting most of the documents of the Socialist

League. *The Manifesto of the Socialist League* (of 30th December, 1884), quoted in the above declaration on the Sudan War, was his also: and it may be worth while to revert to this as typical of the new birth, especially in its opening words:

Fellow Citizens,
We come before you as a body advocating the principles of Revolutionary International Socialism.

On the cover of it (as printed in 1885) is an engraving by Walter Crane of three symbolic figures who sustain a scroll— THE SOCIALIST LEAGUE—and above whose heads are three words "Agitate, Educate, Organise". Below it is stated that the Manifesto, "signed by the Provisional Council at the foundation of the League" on 30th December, 1884, was adopted at the General Conference "held in Farringdon Hall, London on July 6th, 1885": and that this is "a new edition, annotated by William Morris & Belfort Bax". A prefatory note signed by these twain, begins: "The spread of Socialism since the first issue of this Manifesto makes a new edition necessary." Nine months had elapsed since the first issue: an unquenchable optimism was the birthright of these pioneers. On the back page runs the heading: "Literature of the Socialist League", beginning with *The Commonweal* and *The Manifesto* and followed by *Art and Socialism* by William Morris (price 3*d.*) and *Chants for Socialists* by William Morris— "1. The Day is Coming; 2. The Voice of Toil; 3. All for the Cause; 4. No Master; 5. The March of the Workers; 6. The Message of the March Wind. The six poems in one pamphlet, 1*d.*" Then they advertise socialist leaflets and *The Socialist Platform*[1]—seven pamphlets of a uniform size, each embellished

1. The series was to run as follows:
1. *Address to Trade Unions.* By E. Belfort Bax. 1*d.*
2. *Useful Work versus Useless Toil.* By William Morris. 1*d.*
3. *The Factory Hall.* By Edward Aveling and Eleanor Marx-Aveling. 1*d.*
4. *The Commune of Paris.* By E. Belfort Bax, Victor Dave and William Morris. 32 pp. 2*d.*
5. *Organised Labour. The duty of the Trade Unions in relation to Socialism.* By Thomas Binning. 1*d.*
6. *True and False Society.* By William Morris. 1*d.*
7. *Monopoly; or, How Labour is robbed.* By William Morris. 1*d.*

with the same Walter Crane engraving, which are said to be "intended in great measure to be a Commentary on the Manifesto of the League".

Morris turned with great enthusiasm and courage to the building up of a new party. The files of the *The Commonweal* and the letters to his friends give a picture of what now became his main activity. He goes with Eleanor Marx and her husband to a meeting of Oxford undergraduates, thence to meetings in Glasgow and Edinburgh, thence again to meetings in London, speaking all the week-end in the open air at various pitches, sometimes to large audiences, sometimes to the proverbial half-dozen. He is busy writing and proofreading *The Commonweal*, and then selling it in the street. Unlike other well-known men who had given their blessing to socialism, Morris threw himself into the hard, unremitting toil that was necessary to build up a party, because, it should be noted, he understood well that it would be impossible for the working class to win the victory in a revolutionary situation without a strong party. He understood also (for in this he shared the opinion of Engels on lumpen-proletarian riots led by Hyndman) that without a mass movement and a working-class party, strong in its revolutionary theory, there was no possibility of real advance. But though Morris understood this well enough, and understood also many essential features of a revolutionary workers' movement better than many other Englishmen up to the war of 1914–18, he was not in the situation, nor was he himself the man, to build successfully the party that was needed.

Here is no space to give any detailed history of the Socialist League.[1] It was the period when the Fabian and Hyndmanite opportunist tendency amongst the sects was met by a wave of anarchism, amongst whose prominent representatives were Kropotkin in Britain, Domela Nieuwenhuis in the Low Countries and Pelloutier in France.

Within a short time an anarchist wing began to develop in

[1]. With much more fullness than anything hitherto written and with a great intensity of research E. P. Thompson has given the history in his *William Morris: Romantic to Revolutionary* (Lawrence and Wishart, 1955).

the Socialist League. Morris, desperately afraid of a drift back to the opportunist policies of Hyndman, allowed, and even encouraged, the anarchists in the League to gain increasing influence. Engels, who knew well how to fight on two fronts (which Morris did not), and who, along with Marx, had had to leave the Communist Workers' Educational League in the early 'fifties when it began to fall into the hands of the "Putschists", gave his experienced counsel in vain:

> Of the so-called Movement here [Engels writes] I cannot communicate anything good. Hyndman gets more played out every day, he has lost all the trust of his own adherents, but the League is passing more and more into the hands of the Anarchists. . . . Bax and Morris are strongly under the influence of the Anarchists. These men must go through it in *corpore vili*: they will get out of it·somehow; but it is a real piece of luck that these children's ailments are finishing before the masses come into the movement. [Letter to W. Liebnecht of 12th May, 1886][1]

Morris, though never an anarchist, took sides against good elements in the League, those who were making a stand against this epidemic of "children's ailments". The best of these were driven out. The fact is that Morris in the late 'eighties was largely of the same type as those "left" communists with whom Lenin thirty years later carried on a convincing polemic (incidentally taking the title of his book, *Left Wing Communism: an Infantile Ailment*, from just this pungent reference by Engels to the case of Morris and Bax) and by means of this polemic brought them back into a mature understanding of communism. In the case of Morris what Engels had predicted ("they will get out of it somehow") in the end came to pass—as is made clear in his later writings.

The League, after losing the help of Eleanor Marx, got finally into the hands of the anarchists through yielding on Morris's part, and once it became an anarchist body it soon ran upon the rocks. Morris was driven out of the League by the anarchists. Before midsummer, 1890, they had taken

1. See Appendix to this chapter.

from him the editorship of *The Commonweal*. The truth of Engels' prophecy is best related in Morris's own words some years later, when he wrote:

Such finish to what of education in practical Socialism as I am capable of I received afterwards from some of my Anarchist friends, from whom I learned, quite against their intention, that Anarchism was impossible.

At the age of fifty-seven Morris set himself to build a new socialist organisation and composed the manifesto of the Hammersmith Socialist Society, which was the largest branch of the League and which now, in November, 1890, seceded: but there was little he could do. He was rapidly becoming an old man. Four years before this he had written: "I wish I was not so damned old—if I were but twenty years younger."

Hardly had the new society begun when he was prostrated by his worst attack of gout, with disabling kidney disease added thereto. He continued to speak and give lectures, but his most active period was over. But those who, like Mrs. Bruce Glasier in the *Northern Voice* of March, 1934, suggested that he had surrendered to opportunism were simply slandering the memory of Morris. The story was told by the correspondent of *Vorwaerts* that at the funeral of the Russian revolutionary, Stepniak, Morris heard one speaker say that in his later years Stepniak had become more moderate, had abandoned his revolutionary outlook and had come to see the need of Fabian or Liberal methods. Morris was furious. It was a funeral speech, but Morris had no hesitation as he spoke at the grave: "This is a lie," he said, "to suggest that Stepniak had ceased to be a revolutionary. He died as he had lived, a revolutionary to the end."

It was as though Morris already heard the drumming hooves of the asses on his own grave. Within a twelve-month William Morris was dead (on Saturday, 3rd October, 1896). The next week the *Daily Chronicle* contained an article by Bernard Shaw on William Morris as a socialist in which, inevitably, there appeared the words: "He, Morris, practically

38

adopted the views of the Fabian Society as to how the change should come about."

The myth-monger had lost no time in getting to work.

It was forty years later that Bernard Shaw, in his splendid palinode, written at the request of May Morris, took back these suggestions and began his *Morris as I knew him* with the noble words:

> Morris, when he had to define himself politically, called himself a Communist. Very often, of course, in discussing Socialism he had to speak of himself as a Socialist; but he jibbed at it internally, and flatly rebelled against such faction labels as Social-democrat and the like. He knew that the essential term, etymologically, historically, and artistically, was Communist; and it was the only word he was comfortable with.
>
> It must not be inferred that he had any prevision of Soviet technique or any other developed method of Communist organisation. Nobody had, or could have, in his time. He was on the side of Karl Marx *contra mundum.*

ENGELS ON ENGLISH SOCIALISTS

Throughout his overseas correspondence in the 'eighties Engels constantly deprecates the tendency abroad to over-estimate developments in Britain. He himself, as a young German in Manchester, had generously over-estimated the possibilities: fifty years later the old German, now the doyen and guide of European Socialism, warns against being misled by surface appearances, still less by any claims put forward from these "officers-without-an-army". For example, his letter to Paul Lafargue of 20th March, 1886, concludes:

> There is absolutely nothing to do here at the moment. But with Hyndman who knows his way about in crooked politics and is capable of every folly to push himself forward —with H[yndman] on the one hand and our two political innocents [*avec nos deux bébés en politique*] on the other, the prospects are not brilliant—and there the soc[ialist] journals abroad go shouting at the top of their voice that socialism in England is advancing with giant strides! I am very glad that what passes for socialism here is not advancing at all.

Three months later Engels, by this time becoming exasperated with the "political infants" of the Socialist League, writes to Laura Lafargue that he has "had several visits from Bax and one from Morris lately" and says of the latter: "Morris is a settled sentimental Socialist."

It must of course be remembered that in none of his correspondence after the death of Marx does Engels give unqualified praise to any Briton, middle class or working class. Outside the circle of the Marx family, there is no Englishman or Scotsman for whom Engels has really a good word to say. The relative weight of his sardonic comments may be found by putting them in the scales with those on H. M. Hyndman, who is denounced for opportunism, sectarianism, jingoism and treated as an enemy.

CHAPTER FOUR

LETTERS OF WILLIAM MORRIS TO
J. L. MAHON
1884–8

Now that the virulence of the myth has been attenuated in these last thirty years—not by mere passage of time but through the remedial operation of books by Bernard Shaw and others[1]—it is possible to see William Morris as he really was, and in the first place as leader, however much he would have disclaimed it, of a revolutionary socialist organisation. Additional material is now available in fifty letters written by Morris in the last twelve years of his life—his communist years. Of these letters the first thirty (here published for the first time) show Morris in a very interesting light as party worker and party leader, or at any rate as the man who bore chief responsibility for a Marxist organisation. On the other hand letters to Dr. Glasse exhibit Morris in the role of propagandist as well as a lively commentator on current events. As will be seen in the next chapter, these Glasse letters bring out very clearly Morris's standpoint on the much-disputed question of parliamentary action: but in this chapter it is the details of organisational work inseparable from the life of an agitator, the anxieties over the preparation for policy conferences, and such similar matters that are in the forefront.

It was in January, 1883, that William Morris joined the Democratic Federation, which within a few months explicitly adopted socialist principles: a year later it became the Social-Democratic Federation. It was in January, 1884, that a gift of £300 from Edward Carpenter launched the paper *Justice*, to which Morris immediately contributed literary and financial

1. See selected list of books at end of Chapter Six.

support. Morris, then well on in the fiftieth year of his life, had for the past twelvemonth been giving socialist lectures in various parts of the country; and had arranged for one such in Edinburgh. From that city early in March, 1884, a letter suggesting additional meetings was received by Morris, who replied as follows:

> Kelmscott House,
> Upper Mall,
> Hammersmith[1]
> March 13th 1884

Dear Sir

Thank you for your letter: Professor Butcher was good enough to ask me to his house, but I replied that I was engaged to Mr. Glasse; Mr. Campbell must have told you of the engagement he thought probable before he had heard from me: Professor Butcher now asks me to lunch with him on the Thursday, which I shall accept unless you think it would make it impossible to see you or be inconvenient to you indeed. I should not think of leaving without seeing you; that is a matter of course: I will write as you suggest, to Mr. Campbell I suppose. I shall have to return to London by the night mail on Thursday, so shall not be able to accept the invitation from the Symposium.

Please tell me of anything else which would be useful to do, & which I could compass on the Thursday: I propose by the way coming to Edinburgh by the night mail on Tuesday so I should have Wednesday as well for meeting any friends on: only it would I think be better to meet the students *after* the lecture rather than before.

> With best regards
> I am
> Yours fraternally
> William Morris

P.S. I see by the way that there is a train leaving London at 5.15 a.m. which would get me to Edinburgh in time, at 3.30: if this would do I should go by it, because we have an important meeting at the D.F. on Tuesday from which I must not be absent if I can help it: please write.   W.M

1. All the letters to Mahon, with one exception, are from this address.

This was the beginning of a correspondence with John Lincoln Mahon, a young engineer, with whom as yet Morris was not personally acquainted. But, as appears from the letter, he was sufficiently acquainted with leading figures of the Church and learning in the capital of Scotland. John Glasse was the minister of the Greyfriars Kirk where the National Covenant was signed in 1638: he had already shown an interest, unusual at that time, in socialism—and indeed even more unusual in the Scottish ecclesiastical establishment than it would have been amongst the Anglicans south of the Border. The correspondence of Morris with Glasse, as preserved, does not begin till two years after the spring of 1884.

Samuel Henry Butcher, afterwards a Member of Parliament for Cambridge University from 1906 to 1910, had been born in 1850 in the capital of Ireland where his father was Bishop of Meath; and Butcher was afterwards to sit on more than one Royal Commission dealing with University education in Ireland. In 1879 Butcher, in collaboration with Andrew Lang, made a rendering of the *Odyssey* in a prose translation which was to be famous for another half-century. At the time of this letter, and for twenty years afterwards, Butcher was Professor of Greek in the University of Edinburgh: and it may have been a common interest in Homer rather than politics that brought them together. It was two years later in 1886 that Morris began his translation of the *Odyssey*.

In Edinburgh, on Wednesday, 19th March, 1884 (or on the next day), Morris got hold of his new correspondent's name as "MacMahon", but by mid-May had learned to spell it "McMahon". That summer, however, the "Mc" was dropped by its owner.

Mahon, at this time in the nineteenth year of his life, within a few weeks made a "publishing adventure"—really to supply progressive books. On this new business he wrote to Morris and got the following reply:

April 24th 1884

Dear MacMahon

I shall be happy to subscribe £5.0.0. towards the publishing adventure on the distinct understanding that I am

43

not responsible for any debts incurred by the adventure, that it is a loan, I mean, to be repaid at their convenience, or not at all if things go adversely.

I am sorry that I cannot do more at present, (though I may be able as time goes on) but you will readily understand that I am spending a good deal on keeping the agitation on foot here, & I must manage my resources; as, very naturally, Socialists don't seem to be rich generally.

Wishing you all success

I am
Dear MacMahon
Yours fraternally
William Morris

Three weeks later Morris implemented his promise of monetary support and in the same letter raised for the first time the question of "the Land Agitation":

May 13th 1884

Dear McMahon

I enclose the cheque for £5 herewith and wish you all success: your letter did not come up last Tuesday: I should be glad to hear what you are thinking about with reference to the Land Agitation, as it needs some careful steering in dealing with the people who have set it a-going. Of course we dont want to offend them on the one hand; but on the other if people get into their heads that that is all that needs agitating about, it will hinder us greatly.

Yours fraternally
William Morris

A week later, on 20th May, 1884, Morris harks back to the question of "the Land Agitation". This requires some explanation. As is known, Henry George coming from the United States had caused great interest and aroused much enthusiasm by his lectures and his book *Progress and Poverty* which indicated a single tax on land as basic to any solution of social problems. George was not a socialist but he gave an impetus to the growing interest in social questions. H. M. Hyndman, founder of the Democratic Federation, went far beyond George, and so did his followers. There was the same sort of apprehension amongst the socialists that their standpoint would be watered down, if not smothered, by any Land Agitation as there had been an apprehension amongst the Chartists that Cobden's Free Trade League would smother and obliterate the agitation for the People's Charter. Consequently, when the suggestion was made of the formation of a mixed organisation to deal both with the land question and with the labour question, it caused heart-burning and very considerable discussion in the ranks of the Democratic Federation in London. It was ultimately to result in a split in the Federation.

There was, however, much more to it in Scotland at that time than the effect of the Henry George propaganda. There had been a history not only of "landlordism" but a particular grievance, repeated and growing from generation to generation, about the "clearances" or wholesale evictions from the highland glens and from the islands. These "clearances" dated far back: and one of them is the subject of a scathing satire by Robert Burns. The Sutherland clearances of 1819 were particularly mentioned at the time by Walter Scott, and nearly fifty years afterwards by Karl Marx in Volume One of *Capital*. The grievances of the remaining crofters were unabated. They grew to a head in the early 'eighties when in more than one place the military had to be called out in aid of the civil force. The result was that a Royal Commission on the question of the crofts and the crofters was set up in 1883. It reported in 1884 and two years later an Act of Parliament, which still is the main Act governing the crofting tenures to-day, was passed in 1886. While the Royal Commission was at work there was a most extensive agitation going on on this special aspect of the land question.

It is therefore understandable that some of the young socialists in Edinburgh, prominent amongst whom was J. L. Mahon, should have thought that in this existing agitation there was the means to begin rousing the people and that it would lead finally to the road to socialism. The matter was very differently viewed in London. There H. M. Hyndman at once wrote a letter on hearing of this project put forward in the middle spring and took up an attitude of great suspicion towards the proposed Scottish Land and Labour League. It was his view that a branch should straightway be formed of the Democratic Federation and, for the moment, nothing else. Others, however, as will be seen from the following letter, did not share the suspicion entertained by the founder of the Democratic Federation.

May 20th 1884

Dear McMahon
You will probably have heard from Hyndman about your project with the Land people: I heard your letter read when there were some half dozen of us present, and we all agreed that with a man as sound as you are there was no danger, & much chance of advantage in your scheme: we are sure to get *some* of those busy over the land movement, and those that we don't get will I imagine tail off into mere social reformers afraid of their own shadows at every step.

I am going to my publishers this afternoon, & will bid them send you some of my Hopes & Fears for Art on sale or return. I fancy you will sell some in Edinburgh: though written before I had studied socialism from the scientific point of view, they always meant Socialism. Item, I will send you as a gift to yourself my last vol: of poetry in case you care to read it.

Larner Sugden is publishing one of my lectures as perhaps you know: perhaps it might sell with you, though 'tis not as good as the one I gave at Edinburgh.

I return the kind regards and again wishing you all success am

Yours fraternally
William Morris

The second paragraph of the above letter dealt with the book-supply business into which Mahon had plunged. Morris offers on sale or return some of his *Hopes and Fears for Art*, published in 1882. This book was composed of a series of lectures as follows:

"The Lesser Arts" (1877)
"The Art of the People" (1879)

46

"The Beauty of Life" (1880)
"Making the Best of It" (about 1879)
"Architecture in Civilization" (1881)

These were to be sent on sale or return from the publisher Ellis and White, who had put out a second and then a third edition in 1883. Morris also offers Mahon a volume of poetry. This must have been his epic poem *Sigurd the Volsung*.

Two months now elapsed and it was not until mid-July that Morris wrote again, this time in response to some matter of the sales accounts, presumably of *Justice*. It is clear that Hyndman had not merely been suspicious beyond the others of this proposal for a Scottish Land and Labour League, but also had his doubts either about the financial stability or the commercial ethics of the new business man, Mahon, who had started this bookshop. C. L. Fitzgerald was the first editor of *Justice* and H. H. Champion was its publisher. Reference is also made to the fact that Andreas Scheu, the Austrian socialist for whom Morris (unlike Hyndman) had a very high regard, had gone back to Edinburgh.

Scheu was soon convinced by Mahon that it was good to go ahead with the Scottish Land and Labour League. From this moment onwards all the elements for a row inside the Social-Democratic Federation were gathering. At the moment Morris only refers to "many vexations and disappointments of a personal kind", and, for the rest, endeavours to cheer Mahon, who was not finding the path as smooth as he may have hoped.

July 18th 1884

Dear Mahon

I am very vexed that any misunderstanding should have arisen about your account: but it is obvious that Hyndman took his figures from Fitzgerald, & that the latter had made a mistake, which certainly was annoying enough on all grounds, but ought not to upset you too much. As to myself I never had any doubts beyond supposing it possible that you just starting a new business might be hard pressed. In future Mr. Champion will manage all the distribution,

47

and I think it will go better: in fact I am sure it will. Pray understand that I quite know that you are working hard in the cause and have done a great deal.

I am very glad that you see much of Scheu: he has both heart and head, I wish we had a dozen like him: I am sure that he will be the making of the cause in Edinburgh, sorry as I am to lose him from London. I am not the only pecuniary support of Justice; our comrade Carpenter has spent more money than I have on it: however, I suppose I shall have to keep it going now. As Scheu will tell you no one can feel more deeply than I do the necessity for getting rid of all national rubbish; I mean as far as any rivalry goes.

If you come up to London for the Conference I can without any trouble give you a bed, so I hope you will come here then.

In spite of any drawbacks we are certainly moving in London; but one is sometimes appalled at the amount of education that is needed, and it is likely to be a long job: we shall want every man of any energy to work at it: so please excuse my preaching at you to this extent, since I am so much your elder, & older even than Scheu (although he has seen so much more *active service*) that we must put up with many vexations & disappointments of a personal kind, or the cause will push us out of the way to make room for more patient people: meantime I believe you may trust me for always keeping the true principles to the fore whatever my capacity may be.

The philosophical Institution of Edinburgh have asked me to lecture for them: but I would much rather lecture to such an audience as you & Scheu could get me there: at the same time I will not refuse definitely till I hear from you: please write at once as to this. I enclose the copies of the bill you ask for, and am, with best wishes

Yours fraternally
William Morris

P.S. I send a memo: receipt: but you will deal as to Justice with Champion I suppose.   W.M.

P.P.S. You had better distribute the old copies left. W.M.

Your card received thanks.

Two months again elapsed. It is clear from the following letter in mid-September that the enterprise started by Mahon had folded up. Mahon, by August, had gone to Leeds and was looking both for some other place of work and for some other kind of activity than the bookselling. Morris promises to help.

September 13th 1884

Dear Mahon
Thank you for your letters: you may be sure that I impute no blame in the matter of the Edinburgh book-shop. Can you by the way tell Champion of some one to sell Justice both there & at Glasgow.
I will certainly do what I can in trying to find you a place. I am going to Sheffield on the stump in the course of an hour, or I would write at greater length. Hoping to see you soon
I am
Yours fraternally
William Morris

After a month Morris had kept his promise. He had been looking for a place but had not found one in the engineering industry. It is clear that from now onwards he felt some obligation to help Mahon. This would also appear from the tone of both the October and November letters:

October 17 1884

Dear Comrade Mahon
I have been making enquiries about a place but cannot find one at present and there is nothing open in my own business, which I am very sorry for: I will go on trying to find something. Meantime I enclose a cheque for £3, which please accept as a necessity and not as a personal matter between us.
You must tell me what kind of engineering you can do, it is true that I have no influence with the shops here; indeed I am afraid since the foundation of the branch here my name would do you less than good. I quite understand

(as you may easily imagine) what your worries must be under the circumstances.

Hoping all will go well with you

I am
Yours fraternally
William Morris

November 20 1884

Dear Mahon

I send you £1 in case you are in momentary need & will bring you some more tomorrow. I will give you (of course) the recommendation you want for the Museum.

I think Scheu was well pleased with the meeting on Monday at Newcastle: I had a very large audience; some 3000.

Last night was curious: I seemed to feel that George's nostrum was nearly played out; & that a real socialist would have had a good reception. Davitt skated round the subject, & never said anything to favour George's speciality —he was good.

Yours fraternally
William Morris

"George's nostrum" was, of course, the single tax on land already mentioned. Michael Davitt, born in 1846, joined the Fenian brotherhood (Irish revolutionaries) in 1865; was sentenced in 1870 to fifteen years' imprisonment for treason-felony; released on "ticket-of-leave" 1877; founded along with C. S. Parnell the Irish Land League in 1879; was associated to some extent with Henry George and later with the growing Labour movement.

After the autumn of 1884 things developed rapidly towards a split inside the Federation. The quarrel was bound up with the project for the Scottish Land and Labour League now being sustained by Andreas Scheu in Edinburgh. The details of the quarrel, the climax in the month of December, the resignation of the majority of the Council and the formation on the second last day of 1884 of the new Socialist League, are matters of history. They have already been recorded in detail by Morris himself, by his daughter May Morris, by J. W. Mackail, and also by E. P. Thompson, Philip Henderson and by others. The upshot was that J. L. Mahon, aged now nineteen, was appointed first Secretary of the Socialist League. The appointment lasted for some four months. Mahon was very active, as indeed was Morris also, but a quarrel grew up. The upshot of it was the resignation of Mahon, as is explained in the following two letters (one from Morris and one from Mahon to the Provisional Council) and in a resolution which speaks for itself:

May 4th 1885

My dear Mahon

I am sorry to have to say that on the whole I think you would do well to resign your secretaryship. On the other hand I am pleased with you for taking the resolution and admitting that there are reasons for it: for I feel sure that if there is any feeling against you, it is not in the least in the world an ill-natured one, & that you will set yourself right with everybody by resigning. As for any "faults" I dont think anyone, & certainly not I, would be likely to cast them in your teeth; they have none of them been serious in themselves; they have only been inconvenient to the organisation: the truth is the position has been a difficult one, requiring a great deal of arrangement to fill successfully it is no wonder if you didn't quite succeed. If you will take my advice you will cut the matter as short as possible this evening; simply saying that you feel that you find you can't quite get on, that the position requires qualifications which you don't yet possess; that it wants more experience and so on: I mean not to stir up *in the least* any subjects of dispute: everybody will sympathise with you in this case. You should not be discouraged by this matter; you will be able to be useful to the party in many ways, & will be freer to act in some ways that [*sic*] you could be in an official position. I repeat I am pleased that you see the necessity for our going on in a friendly manner; for that doubtless lies at the bottom of your resolution. You may of course reckon on me for doing all I can to assist you.

With best wishes

Yours fraternally
William Morris

26 Clarence St.
Islington
London N.
4th May 1885

To the Provisional Council of the Socialist League

Comrades

I wish to resign the duties of Secretary with which you entrusted me four months ago.

I am sure you will agree that this course is the best for me and for the Council. It is quite evident that we do not get on together as well as a Secretary and Council should. This, I am convinced, is in great measure due to shortcomings of mine which I need not discuss with you at present.

I would suggest, if I may, that my resignation be accepted at once, and with as little discussion as possible. This, I am sure, will tend to help the friendliness between us which I hope will exist in the future,

Yours in the Cause
J. L. Mahon

The Socialist League,
Offices: 27 Farringdon Street,
London, E.C.

That this meeting in accepting the secretary's resignation, records its sense of the earnestness & energy with which he has conducted his duties during his term of office

24/5/85   E. Belfort Bax
C. Mowbray

This resolution, which Mahon had kept together with the letters from Morris, is written on the back of a leaflet issued by the Finsbury Clubs' Radical Association and is headed "Democracy and Disestablishment". The leaflet convenes a London conference of delegates for Wednesday, 6th May, 1885, in support of "Mr. Hopwood's Oaths Bill" and for an expression of "Working Class Radical" opinion on the proposition "That the hour has arrived for the Disestablishment and Disendowment of the Church of England".

Mahon immediately after writing his letter of resignation

of the secretaryship seems to have written suggesting that his friend Tom Maguire of Leeds (also aged about twenty-one) should succeed him in that office. Morris in the next letter replies that he may be a candidate. Actually H. Halliday Sparling (who married May Morris) took on the secretaryship.

May 8th 1885

My dear Mahon

Of course I know nothing of Maguire, except for a letter or two I have had from him which showed sense: of course also I cannot answer his money question you & some of the others might do so: again as to the other questions, they would have to be considered by us in meeting; of course you wouldn't hurry us in going.

I think we must put off consideration till next Monday: I mean to say we can't answer him; he must be considered a candidate subject to certain conditions.

Yours fraternally
William Morris

To the opening months of 1885 there may also be ascribed the following letter, the only one in the correspondence with a heading other than that of Kelmscott House, Upper Mall, Hammersmith:

Morris & Company.
Painted Glass,
"Arras" Tapestry,
Hand-made Carpets,   Merton Abbey,
Furniture Prints,   Surrey,
Damasks, &c., &c.   Friday 1885[1]

My dear Mahon

I forgot like a fool about this Bill; the lecture is to be a special one, & will show how utterly the capitalist would exploit the worker if he could: everybody allowed that it would be a good thing to bill this lecture: so I agreed to tell you to get it printed—& forgot it like an ass.

W. Morris

1. The date is conjectural.

53

After May there is no further letter until the very end of 1885, when Morris had received a request from Mahon that he should come to speak in Leeds where Mahon had now found work. A glimpse is given of the thronging obligations that leadership of the Socialist League had thrust upon Morris:

December 26th 1885

My dear Mahon

I am afraid I shall not be able to manage Jan: look here, engagements (League of various kinds) on 3rd 6th 10th 12th 17th 20th 24th 27th: that doesnt seem to leave much space for you. You had better arrange for a date in Feb: and book me at once: you must remember that going to Leeds & coming back means the heart of 3 days at least. I am glad to hear that you think things look well; I would by all means take a small room: you can't expect to increase the branch without it. If all your 12 men could speak, it would do pretty well: they will have to learn. I am glad also that you have found work: I didn't know that they made guns at Leeds. Yes I am pretty much all right again; can't go a long walk yet, but that will come soon I think. On Monday Bax produced his evergreen resolution of a Weekly Commonweal, after some necessary chaff (Bax wanted it brought out in January). It was agreed that we would start it when we could raise £100: I really think we ought to start it as soon as we can, so I am busy writing cadging letters for cash to everybody that I think good for a guinea. This cadging doesn't concern the country branches as they have more than enough to do to keep themselves going: I think we may bring it out weekly by March. Keep your eyes open and write us things for it fresh and new. The Hyndman muck-heap is going on seething; I am not sanguine about getting rid of his lordship however; humbugs are as hard to kill as cholera-germs.

Thanks for your greetings on behalf of myself—and the Council. The like from me to you and all friends. I thought we looked a little hopeful at our last Monday meeting. The Parliamentary mess could not be going better than it is considering the times.

Yours fraternally
William Morris

Dear Mahon

The numskull post office people have sent back my letter to you (after keeping it a week) with not known on it because I wrote Arnley instead of Armley: damn them! So I send back again as I have nothing fresh to write just yet. I hope you will get my letter this time. Best wishes to you and all friends.

fraternally
W. Morris

In the next letter there is a fairly comprehensive tableau of the prominent personalities amongst the few hundred socialists in London, divided into three warring sects.

It appears that Mahon or the Leeds branch had raised some questions about the leading Fabians. Morris is amused at the suggestion that he had written to Bernard Shaw that "I would punch his head". Shaw at this stage had not yet completely accepted the standpoint of Sidney Webb: and it was some time ahead before Shaw was to reach the intellectual position that he expressed in 1889 in the well-known *Fabian Essay*. Morris, however, thought that Shaw had come "under the influence of Mrs. Besant" and of course it is clear that Annie Besant, who had become so well known as a disciple of the atheist Charles Bradlaugh, M.P., was herself attracted to Shaw at this time. Bradlaugh, however, seems to have remained always a firm anti-socialist. Another stalwart of atheism mentioned was Edward Aveling, who, along with Marx's youngest daughter Eleanor, was prominent in the Socialist League. Morris has heard something to Aveling's discredit: and actually wishes him out of the League and into "the Hyndman muck-heap".

January 15th 1886

My dear Mahon

Many thanks for your letter: mine must be short in return as I am busy (as usual). I am not sure that I can promise the whole week but will do as much as I can: we must arrange definitely further on. I am glad 'tis put off till March, as my old bones don't agree with too much winter travelling. Mrs. Besant? M'm well: I never wrote to Shaw, did I, that I would punch his head? If I did it was a joke. I am still on good terms with him: but, do you know, I came to the conclusion on Wednesday night when he spoke after my lecture & rather defended parliamentarism (as if he were ashamed of himself) that he was rather under the influence of Mrs. B. and on the whole I agree with you that that lady is on the look out for a berth for Bradlaugh, and thinks the Fabian may serve. However I'm glad some people think I'm headstrong. What about B and the Labour statistics bureau? I havn't seen it. Weekly Commonweal. I am trying to collect some money for it, have got some £70, Glasse *not* in it. As to reorganisation the main idea is that we should look after our finances better, I drop the Treasury, and try to get people not to depend on me. The only thing is that I don't see how we can shorten expenses except by giving up our premises, which I cannot do for 2 years or more as you know. If we can make the Weekly Comm: pay its expenses it would be making some use of the place: I mean to say some paying use. I think it a risk but that it ought to be tried: only I cannot and also should not pledge myself to find the money to pay its losses if they are heavy. A circulation of 3000 would cost us a loss of £3 a week 5000 would bring us home. What's your opinion, and could you circulate it up there. Aveling—hem hem! he has been behaving more than queerly to the Woolwich people about some science lessons he was to have given there. They however couldn't quite make a hanging matter of it, and weak attacks strengthen the object of them: so they have dropped it, wisely I think. But I wish he would join Hyndman and let them have a hell of their own like the Texas Ranger. However don't say anything about it.

S.D.F. Family party came off on Sunday last: it must have been "a sweet thing in entertainments". The claque was there in full force, & sung out "go it boss!" when H came on. They settled nothing. How could they? The S.D.F. is Hyndman & Champion. Matters political are flat in London: that damned election has lowered us as I was sure it would. Also the London working men are as a rule a very inferior lot. Meantime trade seems bad enough in all conscience, and it seems probable that the Government are going to put their backs to the wall in the matter of Ireland: fancy that stingy abortion of a Westminster Duke turning truculent! the beggars are getting afraid. Well we must stick to it though I confess that there is plenty of food here for discouragement in the present. Well good luck to you in all ways.

Yours fraternally
William Morris

P.S. Havn't seen your M.S. am afraid it must stand over till next month.

Some solicitude was apparently expressed by Mahon: for in the next letter Morris is "neither ill nor angry, thank you": but extremely busy. As to style of utterance, he echoes Snorro Sturleson in the sagas on "the troubling of kings and scoundrels" and says "unluckily people are so used to rogues and politicians, that when a man speaks plainly they cannot understand him". Meantime he tells that Philip Webb, architect, had become Treasurer of the League. Fred Pickles, mentioned last, was the founder of the Socialist League branch in Bradford.

Mahon's proffered article, like that on the same subject seven months later, would go before Thomas Binning, foreman printer of *The Commonweal*, and afterwards Father of the Chapel at the Kelmscott Press. Binning was also the member of the League responsible for propaganda on trade union matters, on which as Morris writes later that year he had "some quite curious superstitions".

February 7th 1886

My dear Mahon

I am neither ill nor angry, thank you: but am so busy that I am in despair of getting through my work. As to the matter of Commonweal I partly agree and partly not: as I have told you before to write quite plainly & simply what you have to say is the crown of literature, & has not been done in English since the Norman Conquest: still it is what all reasonable men aim at (including myself) who are not rogues or politicians. But unluckily people are so used to rogues & politicians, that when a man speaks plainly

57

they cannot understand him. I should be very glad of your article on the T.U. provisionally I should say that it should not be later at the office than the 18th but I will ask Binning tomorrow.

I think you (the Leeds Branch) were rather precipitate in answering the Fabians: the Council has agreed to send speakers properly furnished with instructions; but will lay the matter before the branches: of course the Fabians ought not to have sent to the branches except through us: at first I scented a plot therein, but I think now it was only stupidity. I don't see why we shouldn't attend this conference and put our own position plainly there. We are in no doubt about our position, and commit ourselves to nothing but what we say there through our delegates: this was the universal opinion up here.

I am very glad that you are so active. I am no longer Treasurer: Webb has taken my place, as on all hands it was thought necessary to pull up as to money matters.

Well I am hurried too so with good wishes

I am

Yours fraternally

William Morris

If you see Pickles tell him I will write to him in a day or two.

It was on 8th February, 1886, that a crowd led by H. M. Hyndman from Trafalgar Square in London broke the windows of the clubs in Pall Mall and also shop windows in Oxford Street. These incidents (recorded in more detail in the Glasse letters in this volume) are "the riots" referred to in the next letter: but not in any detail. Morris was too busy to be able to spare time for a lengthy epistle. He was writing a pamphlet. This, duly advertised in the March, 1886, issue of *The Commonweal* as *A History of the Commune of Paris*, "ready by 15th March", contains some of Morris's noblest writing, particularly in the opening pages. Seven days before the end of February he had found the job "not a little troublesome" and was able to get help (presumably on the military detail) from two collaborators whose names were duly added to the title page. Meanwhile in the pages of *The Commonweal* his serial poem *The Pilgrims of Hope* was reaching its tragic climax amid scenes of the Paris Commune.

February 20th 1886

My dear Mahon

I am sorry; but we must get you to stand over till next month: we have had to get in some articles about the riots. This won't matter for your article as its subject will by no means be stale. I think the article good & straightforward, and it will carry on my idea of "our Policy" which starts this month. I quite agree as to the Trades Unions & think it good to take up that line.

I could write a longish letter if I had time but am desperately busy: have got the job of writing a pamphlet on the Commune to appear by March 18, which I find not a little troublesome.

We are still in a muddle up here and are trying to flounder out of it: don't bully us too much till I tell you it is hopeless, which I don't think it is. Go on working at the branch.

With best wishes

Yours fraternally
William Morris

Morris, a month before the 15th commemoration of the Commune of Paris on 18th March, 1886, was, as we have seen, troubled about the preparation of the pamphlet on it. But after the meeting was held in South Place, near Liverpool Street in London, Morris was very happy, as appears both from a letter written to John Carruthers in Venezuela on 25th March ("a great success, the place crowded") and from the following letter:

March 25 1886

My dear Mahon

I don't see how I can say no after all the talk about it: so be it therefore as to coming. As to subjects there is my lecture called now "Socialism" & which I am to deliver substantially at Dublin as the dawn of a new epoch; I can touch it up & make it serve your turn I think and you may call it the present & future of the working class. My political outlook is a good lecture to people who know something of the subject. And then I suppose you will want an open-air address or something of that kind. I havn't much time to write just now but will do my best. As to your Bradlaugh note, I basely prigged the sense of it and adopted it myself making it much shorter, as was necessary. Commune Meeting as I daresay you have heard a great success. By the by I don't feel sure of the Tuesday as I have to go to Glasgow also, and how I can manage it all I don't know. All right as to my travelling expenses: as to my lodging I will stay with our friend with pleasure.

I am almost afraid that the Fed. have got hold of Kropotkine: at least I am going by Hunter Watts' invitation to meet him tonight. But of course he is an old bird and not easily caught with chaff.

Excuse haste

Yours fraternally
William Morris

The Commune meeting[1] over, there comes a period of nearly four months in which there is only one letter. But this

1. In the celebration of the Commune, held in the South Place Institute, members of all socialist bodies took part: but the initiative had come from the Socialist League. The following resolution was moved by F. Kitz (S.L.) and seconded by Tom Mann (S.D.F.)

That this meeting of International Revolutionary Socialists, assembled in London on the 15th Anniversary of the Commune of Paris, has met to commemorate the heroic devotion of the Parisian working-classes in the Spring of 1871 to the cause of the people, as embodied in that forerunner of the socialised administration of the future—the Paris Commune, and to record its gratitude to those who fell in defence of freedom and the emancipation of labour. That it declares its determination to strive without ceasing for the overthrow in all countries of the system of class-domination founded on force and fraud, and maintained by the folly of the workers, and to establish instead thereof a condition of society based on principles of social justice and international brotherhood. That it fully recognises that the lesson to be learnt from the events of 1871, is that this can only be achieved by simultaneous and organised forcible action, and, therefore, it calls upon the wage workers of the world to unite. Furthermore, it desires to record abhorrence of the malicious lying of the capitalist press with reference to this struggle of the people for their own emancipation.

After tributes had been delivered in German, Italian and French, Eleanor Marx (Socialist League) spoke, followed by P. Kropotkin. Then, "after brief speeches from Headingley (Fabian), Quelch (S.D.F.), Lessner (Communistischer Verein) and Mowbray (S.L.) the meeting ended with the singing of the Marseillaise". (*The Commonweal*, April, 1886) letter is very revealing. Morris by the autumn of 1886 was finding himself in the midst of squabbles of the kind that two years earlier had led to the secession from the Social-Democratic Federation. Some differences were on matters of principle: but others were not, and to such an extent that Morris writes: "I really cannot stand it much longer." Nevertheless, Morris held on week after week until the twenty months' life of the Socialist League had stretched out to thrice that length and more. But from this time on the work of fighting for socialism taxed every ounce of patience and of skill. Morris in this letter gives some hints of his experiences since he had first plunged into active politics ten years earlier. "I now see the absolute necessity of discipline in a fighting body" is his conclusion, with the proviso that this in no sense resembles the conditions of a Communist society. Of great interest also is his attitude to the trade unions which are "not necessarily hostile to socialism". Sir Charles Warren, mentioned in the letter, was Commissioner of the Metropolitan Police.

September 4th 1886

My dear Mahon

Yes please do the Trades Union Congress: I think we ought to take the ground that the Unions are not necessarily hostile to Socialism, and might be made use of when we get to reconstruction: this I fancy you agree with. Your note I weakly suppressed because Binning objected & said that he would have to answer it if it appeared. Though he is sound really on the Unions he has some quite curious superstitions on the subject which fairly puzzle me. For the rest I didn't want to have another controversy in such a very public place as the paper between two Leaguers.

Your letter to the Council was amusing, but I think you have not quite hit the bulls-eye on the matter of the open-air meetings. As to writing to Warren: I voted against it, but saw some reason in it too: because it might have drawn from him an emphatic condemnation of all meetings in the streets, and that would have done us good with the public: and as is now clear it is only by the sufferance of the public, or indeed by their help, that we can hold these meetings at all. On the whole I still think that some of us have made too much of the whole affair: this principally came of our being mixed up with the S.D.F. in the Bell St case. They stuck to Bell St *because* it was a bad pitch; since all they wanted was a row to advertise them and they wanted to do just what we don't want to do, drive the police into a corner.

As to the Council, it really is not so much their fault as the fault of those who want to prevent the Council from acting: what they are driving at I scarcely know, but if they dont look out they will end by breaking up the League. There is such dog-worrying goes on at Farringdon Rd: now that only the sternest sense of duty makes me go there at all: business of course gets neglected amidst all this: They act as though we were a large body with a following of 100,000 at our heels, instead of a sect striving to enmesh a prosylite [*sic*] here and there. I really cannot stand it much longer, the quarrelling is generally about nothing at all: just merely a few people, each one of whom cuts up rough if he don't have *all* his own way. I shall have to withdraw to my own branch and literature if it goes on so. I now see the absolute necessity of discipline in a fighting body, which of course in no sense resembles the Societys of the future. I think we ought to have an executive smaller than the present composed of really picked men, who either agree thoroughly or are quite resolved to keep their points of disagreement in the background and who will stick to business: supplement that by the monthly meetings and constant correspondence with the Branches (detailed at that) and we might get something done. Only the members must make up their minds to abide by the decisions of the Council, and support it, which at present they make no pretence of doing. If this goes on we might as well break up if it were not for the scandal of the thing and the discouragement it would spread. I shall do my level best to hold the League together; but some of the members are so silly, and some so contentious that I think I might as well hold my jaw altogether. Mind you both sides are to blame in these squabbles, so that I really can take service with neither, though of course I put my foot down on the parliamentary business. I can't think what Donald means by that.

I don't know if you heard of me & the S.D.F. Lane thinks they want me to join them again; they have excommunicated the League—which I think a good job.

I shall be in town till Friday and can give you a bed if you will come over: I shall be very glad to see you.

Yours fraternally

William Morris

Eight months later forebodings about differences leading to schism have been realised. The Council of the Socialist League in the autumn of 1886 had been trying to reach an agreed policy on the question of participation in parliamentary elections. It was in vain. So the main and growing conflict in London in the early months of 1887 was between "parliamentarians" and "anti-parliamentarians". Meantime J. L. Mahon had been carrying on an agitation in the big cities and in the coalfields which reached a climax of successful meetings amongst the Northumbrian miners. Morris, delighted with this activity of Mahon, with its results in organisation that seemed solid enough at the time, agreed to go to Northumberland where in April, 1887, he found some of the most responsive audiences he had ever addressed.

The 3rd Annual Conference of the Socialist League was now approaching. It was to be held at Whitsuntide on 29th May, 1887, and was preceded by a fierce discussion and much canvassing of opinions amongst the members. The Croydon branch headed by Belfort Bax proposed that every available means of realising the objects of the League should be pursued, "parliamentary or otherwise".

At this moment Morris became aware that Mahon, who had been a strong "anti-parliamentarian" in the autumn of 1886 and even in the beginning of 1887, had swung right over. Mahon had been convinced by his experiences among the Northumbrian miners and elsewhere of the need for a change in policy. Morris himself had been in favour of deferring decision for another twelvemonth. These anxieties are reflected in the following letters.

May 5th 1887

My dear Mahon

I dont agree with your optimistic views about the Conference. I think there will be a split in fact: because if we carry our resolution your side will do nothing to help the League; & if you carry yours some of our best men will leave it: and as to myself I shall only belong to it in name & shall probably soon be driven out of it altogether; as I don't see how I can belong to a body advocating a set of "stepping stones", in which none of us really believes. In any case one thing is certain as a result of the parliamentary move, i.e. the extinction of Commonweal. In the lightness of your heart you may say that doesn't matter; but I can't agree with you; any new paper started will have to make its way up to the point at which the old one was stuck. As to the declaring ourselves collectivist no one is likely seriously to object to that, as every one can interpret that idiotic name as he best pleases. You talk of one branch being parliamentary & another not: that is nonsense: the new Council (if the res: is carried) will speedily expel any branch which does not accept the parliamentary programme which they will be bound to produce; and from their point of view, rightly so. The whole League and every member of it will be bound by a resolution affirming the necessity for parliamentary action, which is a distinct change of policy on the part of the League: and as it can only change its policy in the S.D.F. direction, I don't see the use of its existing as a separate body if that change takes place. So I hope your side will be beaten, since no compromise seems possible. As to the success at Blythe, of course it must come to the miners joining one body or another or else doing nothing in propaganda. May all turn out better than I fear.

Yours

W. Morris

To this letter, eleven days later (as appears from an annotation upon it in J. L. Mahon's handwriting), an answer was sent, on 16th May, 1887. This brought an immediate lengthy reply from Morris who is very perturbed about the possible outcome of the approaching annual conference of the League.

My dear Mahon

I dont suppose any body wants to get rid of me out of the League: but I may be obliged to leave it for all that. Bax stated to me explicitly that if the Croydon Branch's resolution were carried, the new Council on meeting would at once proceed to draw up a parliamentary & palliative programme. I told him that this ought to be put into the resolution, and he agreed and said it should be done if possible: nor can I see any other possible outcome of the declaring, either in the Croydon resolution or in yours, for parliamentary action. Now if you will turn to the 1st weekly number of the Commonweal you will find what I then thought of this matter which was signed by Bax never called in question by any one in the League, and *which is still my opinion*. I should have been contented with the acceptance of the Ham: compromise of letting the matter alone for a year, if it could be carried out; but it seems that that cannot be done, therefore there is nothing for it but to oppose a direct negative to the Croydon resolution; and as the League will not be the body that I joined if the programme in question is sanctioned by it, I shall then have to leave the league, though I would not do so merely for the passing of a vague resolution as far as I can see at present. You see the matter is very simple: the branches, you say, are all parliamentary; if so I do not agree with them, & therefore cannot help them in making what I think a blunder without being in plain terms a liar, which I do not choose to be. As to your amendment, it might mean either one thing or another; if passed it would leave us where we were, and fighting as to the meaning of the sentences: whatever we pass should be clear either for the new departure, or against it, or for shelving the discussion of it. If you are in favour of sending socialists to Parliament without a palliative programme (an absurdity to my mind) this ought to be stated. If you think that one branch might act parliamentary, & another abjure such action, this also ought to be stated. (Of course there need be no central body in that case beyond a literature committee.) You see once more if you dont intend the league to put up parliamentary candidates with a programme which they are to try to carry, I cannot see why you should make all this pother; why you shouldn't let us go on as we have been going on till some kind of action is forced upon us: we should gradually shake off the quarrelsome part of our "ways & manners" and settle down to what (I think) is our work, getting the workmen to organize genuine revolutionary labour bodies not looking to parliament at all but to their own pressure (legal or illegal as the times may go) on their employers while the latter lasted. I am at least sure that this must be done whether socialists go in for parliament or not.

For the rest I am, as you very well know, more averse than anybody to the breaking up of the League. In fact I must say plainly that the knowledge that this is so has been played on by the "parliamentary section" who, I cannot help thinking, would not have gone so far if they had understood that I cannot be driven further than a certain point. I do not complain of this, as I believe it is at least as much my fault as that of other persons, but I state it.

Finally you must not forget that whatever open steps I might take, I personally would have nothing to do with politics properly so called. The whole business is so revolting to a decent quiet body with an opinion of his own, that if that were our road, I should not be able to help dropping off it.

Finally 2nd. If you (I mean plural) are in earnest in not wanting a palliative programme you can set us right on that point by pledging yourselves against such programme, in which case the whole damned dispute will come to an end and we shall be able to get to work.

As to being anxious about the matter, I am naturally somewhat anxious; since if things go at the worst it is a case for me of beginning again. However I hope they won't and shall as a matter of course do my best to get people to agree to some course of action without dividing (I mean voting) on the matter.

Yours
William Morris

After the defeat of the "parliamentarians" in the Socialist League Congress at the end of May, 1887, Mahon and others formed a "cave" which sought for a Special Conference.

Engels, who was consulted, was opposed to this—as appears from his correspondence[1] with F. A. Sorge in New York. Meanwhile Mahon had organised in Northumberland a new body, a North of England Socialist Federation, and sent a report of it to *The Commonweal*—dealt with by Morris in the opening sentence of the next letter:

June 14th 1887

My dear Mahon

I will put the N of E S.F. in next week's issue: it is too late for this: I must of course make a remark about the programme. Pray do your best for Commonweal up there: this will be of use to you, you know, against the day when Aveling gets it out of my hands. I am sorry to say that your writing to the Bloomsbury Branch seems to have done no good: Donald, challenged as to the money collected as you were, instead of referring us to the B.B. as you rightly did, set on the Sec: of the B.B. to write a letter which was ill-mannered, impudent & evasive: however the Council took it very coolly, & simply asked the B.B. to explain the matter further. Still we cannot submit to the B.B. claiming to boss the League. Send the articles & I will see I can't

1. "No movement absorbs so much fruitless labour as one which has not yet emerged from the status of a sect. You know that just as well as I. At such times everything turns to scandalmongering. And so once more my letter is about English affairs.

"The Sunday before last saw the conference of the Socialist League. The anarchist element, which had been allowed to get into it, and is supported by Morris (who hates everything Parliamentary like poison, is hopelessly muddle-headed, and as a poet is above science), have won. A resolution, seemingly innocuous, to the effect that *to-day* there can be no talk of Parliamentary action, was passed by 17 votes to 11 . . .

"But in reality, the decisive circumstance was Morris's threat to leave the League if any kind of parliamentary struggle be recognised in principle. And as Morris covers the weekly £4 deficit of *The Commonweal*, that outweighed all else by far.

"Our people now want to organise the provinces, and after three or four months to call an extra-ordinary congress to overthrow the decision. That would be a failure. In the manufacture of voting sections the anarchists are far better than our people, and can make seven men into eight voting sections. But the comedy has its good aspects, and with the presence of the workers in the League it is not to be ignored. Naturally, Bax is with us, and from the workers, Donald, Binning, Mahon and others—the best. None of our people stood for election to the Executive Council." (4th June, 1887.)

tell beforehand can I? At the same time I dont want to make the Commonweal sectional so I will probably put them in. As to the subscription—No. Not that I couldnt find the money or that I grudge it to Donald (though I think he has behaved very ill throughout) but that I think it better to give what I do give through the League's treasurer, & henceforward shall not give anything except that way. I don't think things will go smooth, but rather that the League will disappear if a special conference is called, & you beat us of course that will end it, which I think will be a pity. I shall do my best to keep what remains of it together, & work in London all I can; not because of any theory but because it lies near my hand. If the League does disappear, I shall try to get a dozen men together whom I can trust, & who have definite ideas about socialism and decline anybody who doesn't really hold these views: I will speak & write wherever I can: but I will not give one penny to support any set of people who wont come up to the test.

Lastly to you personally get into work if you can & dont become a hack of any party.

Yours very truly
William Morris

Three days later Morris gives an account of the Fabians whom he is beginning to recognise as the real theoretical opposition to his own standpoint. There are pen-pictures of the Fabians. Hubert Bland, husband of Evelyn Nesbit, is described as an "offensive snob"—a description which accords with the writer's own recollection (of fifty years ago) of a monocled Bland revealing himself as a Bismarckian State-Socialist. For the rest Morris's description bears out what Engels said of the Fabians at that time that they (including Bernard Shaw) were "high-nosed" (*hoch-nasige*).

June 17th 1887

My dear Mahon

All right about the Commonweal: that would be very useful. I can't see any objection to your proposal if you think it likely that you will get rid of 6 quires & upwards as I suppose you would. In any case tis worth trying. The programme in this week with a mild word from me. The debate at the Fabian last night was a very absurd affair only enlivened by a flare up between me & that offensive snob Bland: otherwise I was as mild as muffin's milk, & I think rather more coherent than anybody else, except Mrs. Besant, who spoke in her usual "superior person" style. Shaw was bad & languid, but also "superior". He has once again got a pocket full of conundrums which he pulls out from time to time: his real tendencies are towards individualist-anarchism. Well this is gossip— So good luck.

Yours

W. Morris

P.S. Once again I think (if you will excuse advice) that you had better settle down in Newcastle and nurse your new Socialists there.

Ten days later a letter begins by upbraiding Mahon for being "unbusinesslike" about the sales of *The Commonweal*: and is followed the next day by another letter warning about the danger to the paper as a weekly, and also giving political advice to Mahon:

July 26th 1887

My dear Mahon

The note about Federation shall go in; & I will hand in your letter to the W. & M. I must say I consider it bad business, because it comes to this that the papers which you professed to have sold were really disposed of gratis: it is this kind of thing which is sinking Commonweal, and I cannot see why you should not have sent up the money for the copies actually sold, which is all that we can expect any one to do: it is excessively stupid of us to be unbusinesslike. Well in return do please try to collect some money for Commonweal: if we can't get a good deal together it will not live through the autumn, I mean as a weekly.

I heard a rumour that Donald is going to Birmingham to agitate not for the League but for the "Midland Socialist Federation". Is this true? If it is, it shows treachery I should not have thought Donald capable of though I dont rate his morals high. I don't know whether you think I have any right to give you advice, but Birmingham brings Sketchley to my mind, & I hold him out to you as a warning as a man who has to live on the party by—well by cadging. I think that a bad business, and strongly advise you to get to your work again & stick to it for fear you might drop into that line. Its all very well for a time, at some special crisis to do as you have been doing; but it can't last in a reasonable way. It is perhaps possible that the party might at some time or other have paid lecturers, but I dont know; anyhow it cannot keep them now.

I am sorry I didn't meet you when you were in town, as I should have said this to you instead of writing it. Wishing you luck & again begging you to do your best to save the Weal from extinction.

I am

Yours truly

W. Morris

July 27 1887

My dear Mahon

Other article received with thanks. As to our sending to Northumberland, I think if we are sending anyone anywhere it should be to recruit for the League definitely. You have set the Northumbrians going with the help of literature & an occasional visit they ought to be all right. I was in doubt at the time about the expediency of starting a new organisation there; I now think it was a mistake and that it would have been better to let the S.D.F. take over if we (the League) could not. In fact in no spirit of hostility I recommend the parliamentary section of the League to join the Federation: you would be powerful there, & would be able to prevent such follies as you are telling me about: of course I say this on the assumption that your section is irreconcilable.

We are sending out subscription cards for Commonweal which please note if we can't get them pretty well filled up 'tis all over with the weekly issue.

Yours truly

William Morris

Advice to Mahon from an older man seems to have been like a red rag to a bull. So three days later Morris writes to the offended Mahon placably enough: but it is clear that Morris has been thoroughly put out by the behaviour of Mahon's friend, the young A. K. Donald:

July 30 1887

My dear Mahon

Knowing my friend, I rather expected you to be offended by my last letter if you are speaking of that in which I was so rash as to offer you advice. But I cannot say that I think I was severe: or that your explanation makes matters better. I fail to see why the struggling Commonweal should be fined because the Strike Committee thought it inadvisable to keep you on as an emissary in the North. It seems to me as if this were dis-organisation rather than organisation. Of course I admit that you acted for what you thought the best: but lord! if we all take to the same game why should we take to an organisation at all? This is anarchism gone mad. I admit cheerfully your capacity for hard work in the movement, & have always praised you for it: *but* (here comes the knock on the nose to me) I have always thought that though you were good at propaganda, you had a knack of setting people by the ears only second to Donald's. Only you see he likes it, & I don't know that you do: all this I don't think is fruitful of organisation. As to Donald, I am pleased that you should stand up for your friend; and also pleased to hear that he is not engaged on the nefarious transaction I heard of. You will observe I asked you to contradict it, but I admit I ought to have asked him: I will do so next time. As to his general morals that was partly a joke which even a half Scotch-man cannot be expected to see: but also as you admit later on he does not profess a high standard and people must expect to be taken at their own valuation. As to brags about the relative amount of work we do; let's remember the old proverb and wait till we are dead before we raise that question— and meantime do all we can. Yes, please consider my advice not because it's mine, but because it's good. For my part I don't like the idea of professional agitators, & think we ought to be able to do without them: but at any rate no *loose* organisation can manage with them; they must be employed either by a well organised body, or by some private person, and be either kept in very strict order, or be perfectly free to go their own ways. As to looking at you with suspicion. I think I know what you will do up there, almost as well as if I were with you, and I think you will do some good and some harm: my hope is that the good will much over balance the harm: there is no room for suspicion, since I know all about it.

I am not in the least in an ill-temper, but I am vexed that the road to *organisation* should lie through the breaking up of the League, and the snuffing out of Commonweal, if that must be so. However I shall go on with my work as if that were not to be, and perhaps we may escape by the skin of our teeth.

Fraternally & good temperedly yours
William Morris

Of what followed thereafter there is no record in letters. But six or seven weeks later Mahon had made some complaint which brought down upon him Morris's wrath in the following letter:

September 21st 1887

My dear Mahon

You are in some respects a very foolish young man and overwhelmed with the idea of your own importance, or I should be angry with you. But as I have really been on friendly terms with you, and also since I have known all about you from the first, and have never expected more than I have got out of you, it would not be fair of me to turn round on you as if your little ways were a surprise to me: therefore I answer your letter as a proof that I think no worse of you than I did, except perhaps that you have turned out a little more quarrelsome than I expected.

I have never written or communicated to any one of the Edinburgh people since I was last in Scotland at which time, as you had not become so great a man as you are now, your name was not mentioned I believe.

I write & receive letters from Glasier sometimes, but I dont remember ever mentioning your name to him or he to me. In a letter I had from him not long ago he expressed, what many of us feel, annoyance at the shoving forward of the name "Scottish Land & Labour League": but I advised him to take no notice of it, since the Edinburgh people were stirring in some direction. Otherwise the subject matter of our letters has been the general affairs of the League & of his own Branch, & as far as I am concerned you or anybody else are perfectly welcome to read my letters.

So you see my dear Mahon, that it is probably your own manners & ways that have drawn this opposition on you; indeed I have noticed, that though I think you are good natured enough, you do always seem to have a genius for setting people by the ears; doubtless without intending it. Anyhow nothing that I have said can have had anything to do with it as to your friends I have said nothing. At the same time I have of course criticised you in conversation among our friends up here: do you by any chance consider yourself to be above criticism? I don't think you can complain of my usage of you in the C. either; I have stuck in any thing you have sent me in the way of notices &c and have let you advertise your S.L. & L.L. as much as you pleased. Well—there—you must believe or not as seems good to you when I say that I have said the worst that I have said *of* you *to* you. As to metropolitan ways, I must tell you that we have got very peaceable in the metropolis, and if you or others dont stir up the quarrel again I think it is likely to drop—which would be a great blessing.

Now please to lay by your unreasonable suspicions, which are not worthy of a brisk young chap like you, & do your damnedest against the enemy, and sell Commonweal all you can: I agree with you in thinking it very foolish to think that you or anybody can nobble the movement.

Your article is rather short & rough for such an important subject, but I will print it, as it is all right as far as it goes, and I agree with its suggestions.

By the way I believe now I think of it that I *have* written to Tuke since the Conference; but I dont think there was any controversial matter in the letter. I mention this lest your suspicions should be again aroused. You may show my letter to anybody you please, or any letters I write to you.

Wishing you success, and calm.

I am
Yours fraternally
William Morris

Three weeks later Morris writes once more and in a very kindly mood. But this is the last of the regular correspondence:

October 14th 1887

My dear Mahon

I am sorry, but it is really impossible for me to make the northern tour this autumn. I have several engagements, and for the rest I really cannot afford the time, or indeed the money: for business is slack, and my chance of not being driven into a corner lies in my working at it hard personally. I shall hope to be able to come north in the spring, & perhaps I should be as useful then as now. I am glad to hear that you are doing so well: but please get the Branch to *pay regularly* (I don't know if they owe much). If you can get them to do that and sell additional numbers (as you are doing) it will be better than donations. I will speak to Binning about his notes. I am in hopes we shall yet turn our backs on our quarrels; only there is one not back but Bax who is being steeped in the Marxite pickle over at Zurich who I fear will want some sitting upon when he returns. It would be very foolish to let him embroil everything again merely to get a compact adherence to the German Social Democrats.

Fraternally
W. Morris

Six months later, in the spring of 1888, there is one more letter. Mahon had become interested in the Mid Lanark by-election which marked the rejection by the Liberal Party organisation of the Liberal candidature of Keir Hardie, who then persisted in standing for election independently of the party organisation. Keir Hardie afterwards joined with R. B. Cunninghame Graham, M.P., to form, in 1888, the Scottish Labour Party—a forerunner of the Independent Labour Party of five years later. Morris is curt about Hardie: but ends the letter to Mahon on a friendly note:

April 3rd 1888

My dear Mahon

Thanks for your letter & explanation; I have no sort of quarrel with you, though I disagree with your tactics

74

partly: I don't want to contend with any one whom I believe to be sincere in pushing any side of Socialism or even democracy; if I have had any contention with persons whom I believe to be genuine it has been because I have wanted the S.L. not to be swamped under the general flood of opportunism, which I will not deny is necessary. Outside the League I have no contention with any one who is attacking the present society: inside I must contend, though mostly in a friendly way, against those who would make the League parliamentary & opportunist.

You no doubt will be ready to admit that you have made some mistakes in your Northern propaganda, and *I* believe on the other hand that you have done much service in agitation there. I am glad to hear that you are going to get to your work (grind) as I don't see how the party can pay for agitators & organisers from its present poverty. About Keir Hardy I know nothing: his candidature will only be useful I think for raising a rumpus and splitting the liberal party.

Wishing you luck in all ways

I am
Yours fraternally
William Morris

P.S. If ever you come up to town I shall be glad to see you.

There is no record of letters from or of visits to Morris after this: and, apart from an Engels-Mahon correspondence[1] in the later 'eighties, there are no outstanding published letters. But for several more years Mahon was active with one venture after another. In 1888 there appeared *A Labour Programme* by J. L. Mahon, a 100-page pamphlet with a lengthy preface by R. B. Cunninghame Graham, M.P.

Although Mahon was present at an early I.L.P. conference, when it came to the General Election of 1895 he was not one of the twenty-eight I.L.P. candidates who (together with four candidates from the Social-Democratic Federation—among them George Lansbury) suffered electoral defeat along with Keir Hardie. At Aberdeen, where he received 608 votes, Mahon stood as a "Labour" candidate.

1. E. P. Thompson, *op.cit.*, Appendix II.

In his later years Mahon, by this time domiciled in London, devoted much attention to the memory of Morris. The Kelmscott Fellowship with May Morris as president was inaugurated on 13th March, 1918: and a year later Mahon was added to the Fellowship's committee of ten members. He played a considerable part in the preparation and publication (at the Twentieth Century Press in September, 1919) of *The Commonweal* "founded by William Morris in 1885: New Series No. 1". There never was a second number. Thereafter Mahon was always ready to help in any way connected with William Morris. He married in his early twenties. His son, John, after a period in the workshop, became a leading figure in trade union and political activity and for the last sixteen years has been the secretary of the London District of the Communist Party.

J. L. Mahon, who was born on 8th June, 1865, as McMahon, had between the age of eighteen and thirty played a not inconsiderable part in the growth of the socialist movement. He died on 19th November, 1933.

CHAPTER FIVE

LETTERS OF WILLIAM MORRIS TO
DR. JOHN GLASSE
1886–95

MORRIS was a guest-friend of Dr. Glasse in Edinburgh from the first time that he went up and down the island, giving lectures on socialism; that is, from the spring of 1883 onwards. But the extant letters Morris wrote to his friend (made available by Dr. Glasse's daughter in 1951) do not begin until three years later, in the spring of 1886. All are addressed from Kelmscott House, Upper Mall, Hammersmith.

Dr. John Glasse had been attached to the Social-Democratic Federation whence he had gone into the Socialist League. He was the minister of the Old Greyfriars Parish Kirk, in which the Covenant of 1638 had been subscribed and in whose kirkyard, forty years later, over a thousand Covenanters had been confined for months in a primitive concentration camp. He was born in 1848. The present writer remembers him, when he was nearing sixty, as a man with a noble brow and an aureole of silver hair who gave greeting and countenance to a number of young socialists at a gathering one evening in Edinburgh. Glasse, in the recollection of an old member of the S.D.F. who joined the Edinburgh branch in 1906, remained true to the outlook of the Socialist League, and, though he did not attach himself formally to either I.L.P. or S.D.F., could always be relied upon for help in difficulties.

Glasse's later writings included *John Knox, a criticism* (1905) and a couple of other books published after his death in 1918. His earlier writings included *Pauperism in Scotland, past and present*; *Robert Owen and his life work*; *Modern Christian Socialism*;

The Relation of the Church to Socialism. Many of his writings are as yet unpublished.

It was with Glasse that Morris stayed when his tours of agitation took him to Edinburgh, as Morris tells in a letter to his daughter Jenny:

> . . . So to Edinburgh with a nice innocent comrade of that branch, Gilray,[1] who dropped in upon me the day before: you know one has about 30 minutes sea from Fife across the firth to Granton, whence of old times I set sail to Iceland. I stayed [with] Glasse at Edinburgh and had a meeting in the evening (Tuesday, 5th) not very well attended, but interesting because it seems the audience was a new one, and a good [?deal] hostile so that Glasse was afraid of putting our resolution, which however we carried after a rather stormy debate, owing to the stupidity of a cut and dried opponent one Job Bone, who always opposes everything, and is known in Edinburgh as the "Bone of Contention". [14th April, 1887]

The first letter is dated little more than a year after Morris, heading a majority of the Council of the Social-Democratic Federation, had founded the Socialist League. The new body at this stage had the support of Frederick Engels. Hyndman, leading the Council's minority that retained the title of Social-Democratic Federation, plunged into adventurous courses that would bring publicity. The rest of the background to this first letter is shown clearly in correspondence[2] between Engels and Bebel, the leader of the German Social-Democratic Party. On 15th February, 1886, Engels writes that the Social-Democratic Federation "which, despite all self-advertising reports, is an extremely weak organisation" was brought "to the verge of dissolution" at the November, 1885, general election, when Hyndman "had taken money from the Tories" and with it put up Social-Democratic candidates in two London constituencies, where they got thirty-two and twenty-seven votes respectively. Three months later, on 8th February, 1886, H. M. Hyndman led "a procession of 'unemployed'

1. John Gilray died at the age of ninety-four in 1951.
2. *Marx-Engels Selected Correspondence*, edited by Dona Torr, 1934.

through Pall Mall, the street of the big political, aristocratic and high-capitalist clubs". When the "aristocrats at the club windows sneered at them, they broke the said windows, ditto the shop windows". Afterwards, these "masses of the Lumpen-proletariat, whom Hyndman had taken for the unemployed", streamed through the West End, "looted jewellers' and other shops", and then dispersed. It is with this West End riot of 8th February that Morris's first letter deals.

February 10, 1886.

My dear Glasse,
Thank you very much. I know that you will do what you can in spreading the light. As to Monday's riot, of course I look at it as a mistake to go in for a policy of riot, all the more as I feel pretty certain that the Socialists will one day have to fight seriously because though it is quite true that if labour could organise itself properly the enemy could not even dream of resisting, yet that organisation could not possibly keep pace with the spread of discontent which will accompany the break up of the old system, so that we shall be forced to fight. Well, it is a mistake to try to organise riot; yet I do not agree with you that Monday's affair will hurt the movement. I think it will be of service: any opposition to law and order in the streets is of use to us, *if the price of it is not too high;* in this case I don't think it will be; the worst part of it being that it rather rehabilitates Hyndman: if they try him it will be a misfortune from that point of view: but I don't think they will. I believe by the way from all I hear that the outbreak was a surprise to the interviewer. I don't think there was much *exaggeration* in the papers, but considerable misstatement. The mass of the crowd, from what I can hear (I was not present), was composed of workmen, but of course there were bound to be a certain number of professional thieves (who after all are a necessary product of our Society). For the rest an English mob is always brutal at any rate till it rises to heroism. Altogether taken I think we must look upon this affair as an incident of the Revolution, and so far encouraging: the shop wrecking was partly a grotesque practical joke (quite in the English manner) at the expense of the upper classes. At any rate it is a glimpse for them of

79

the bed-rock of our present society, and I hope they like it. Yesterday they were gibbering with terror in spite of the sham calm heroics of the newspapers. I shall say frankly what I think about the affair in the next C., *must* in fact.

Yours fraternally,
William Morris

In the next *Commonweal* (journal of the Socialist League, issued from February, 1885, onwards), Morris as editor duly issued a statement of policy in which he put forward the hope for "a strong party, educated in economics, in organisation, in administration"; but, perhaps with a side-glance at the newly formed Fabian Society, stated: "We must be no mere debating club, or philosophical society; we must take part in all really popular movements when we can make our own views on them unmistakably clear; that is a most important part of the education in organisation." He ends with summing-up "our policy" in three words—"Education towards Revolution".

Over a year elapses before the next letter in which, amongst League matters, there is a reference to "your Odyssey". Morris, it would seem, had promised Glasse a copy of *The Odyssey of Homer done into English verse*, the first volume of which had been published early in April.

April 14, 1887.

My dear Glasse,

After all I stayed in Scotland till Sunday, as I was so earnestly pressed to assist at the Easter Monday meeting in Northumberland. It was a capital meeting, and there is no doubt that Mahon has done well there, and that the movement has taken hold. I send you a copy of the *N. Chronicle* which has a good report of Hyndman's and my speech but has omitted Donald's which was very good. The Easter Monday in London was a great triumph for the Socialists at any rate.

I send you the leaflet mentioned by me; Binning at the League will deal with you if you want any; it is now called "What the Socialists want".

I am not forgetting your Odyssey.

Don't forget that we ought to have a delegate from the Branch up at Whitsuntide.

Yours ever,
William Morris

The 1887 Annual Conference of the Socialist League was now approaching and Morris was uneasy about it, lest a decision be taken about "parliamentary action" which might be a throw-back to the tactics which had been such a discredit to the Social-Democratic Federation.

These tactics by which, in the two London constituencies contested at the 1885 General Election, they had received a ludicrous total of less than sixty votes, were obviously a blunder. Place and time were both wrong, conditions were not ripe (the seed was hardly sown) and from the point of view not only of Morris but also of Engels, it was done by the wrong people. But Morris then went to the other extreme. He conceived such a dread of the corrupting influence of the Westminster Parliament that he came out against present participation in it or in electoral activities concerned with it. He felt that the small band of socialists and the workers they influenced should ignore Parliament till a very much later stage: but in taking this standpoint he himself ignored the need of the workers to *experience* all the good and all the bad that could come from Parliament. Morris, however, took this leftist standpoint, which invited the retort of the old Russian proverb: "If you are afraid of wolves, don't go in the woods."

With his mind thus beset by fears, Morris pressed for Glasse, who had been one of his main supports, to come up for the Conference which fell at Whitsuntide on 29th May.

May 19, 1887.

My dear Glasse,

Am I to have the pleasure of seeing you in London at Whitsuntide? I hope so. If so you understand of course that you will come to my house, and I need not say that we shall be glad to see Mrs. Glasse also. My wife has now returned from Italy and will be pleased to know her.

I am very uneasy anent the Conference. The parliamentary people are looking like driving matters to extremity, which means driving me out of the League if they succeed. I am quite ready to let the matter rest if they will really leave it alone, but I cannot support a "Stepping-Stone" policy which for me (since I don't believe in them) would mean acting a lie.

I hope your people will be prepared to support the mild negative which the Hammersmith Branch will move, in case the question comes up for discussion. I have no wish to quarrel with the S.D.F. but I cannot swallow my words and rejoin them; and to have two organisations holding the same tenets and following the same policy seems to me absurd.

Of course if any other comrade comes up with you I shall be very glad to house him.

With best regards to Mrs. Glasse.

> Yours very truly,
> William Morris

Glasse, however, was unable to come; and in the next letter Morris sets forth to him very clearly his standpoint on the function and limitations of the parliamentary activity of a socialist party.

> May 23, 1887.

My dear Glasse,

Of course you are quite right not to shove your head into the noose: I by no means approve of men running to meet martyrdom. I shall hope to see you later on in the year, when I suppose you will be coming to London. Will you kindly forward to Tuke the accompanying note, so as to put him at his ease as to coming to a strange house.

My position to Parliament and the dealings of Socialists with it, I will now [try] to state clearly. I believe that the Socialists will certainly send members to Parliament when they are strong enough to do so: in itself I see no harm in that, so long as it is understood that they go there as rebels, and not as members of the governing body prepared by passing palliative measures to keep "Society" alive. But I fear that many of them will be drawn into that error by the corrupting influence of a body professedly hostile to Socialism: and therefore I dread the parliamentary period (clearly a long way ahead at present) of the progress of the party; and I think it will be necessary always to keep alive a body of Socialists of principle who will refuse responsibility for the action of the parliamentary portion of the party. Such a body now exists in the shape of the League, while germs of the parliamentary side exist in the S.D.F., Fabian and Union. Now why should we try to confound the policy of these bodies? The opinion, or if you please sentiment, will exist in any case, and must at some time or another give rise to definite organisations. I appeal to those who doubt the usefulness of such a body of principle at all events to stand aside and not to break it up but join other bodies now existing for whom I for my part feel complete tolerance, so long as they are not brought *inside* ours. But if that is done the League will sooner or later be broken up, because, I repeat, the non-parliamentary feeling will assuredly not be repressed entirely.

All this has nothing to do with the question of Collectivism or Anarchism; I distinctly disagree with the Anarchist principle, much as I sympathise with many of the anarchists personally, and although I have an Englishman's wholesome horror of government interference and centralisation which some of our friends who are built on the German pattern are not quite enough afraid of I think. I agree that it would be not so much impolitic as impossible to pronounce on the matters of religion and family. People's instincts are I think leading them in the right direction, in these matters, and yet the old superstitions, as they have now become, have such a veil of tradition and literature about them it is difficult to formulate the probabilities (they can be no more) of the new order in words that will not be misunderstood, and so cause offence.

As to *my behaviour* in this difficult crisis, I can only say that I do not feel the least bitterness to anyone, and shall do my best to get people to find a peaceable solution for present trouble, or even to accept a staving off loyally and with single heart. But indeed I cannot go on nagging for ever. I loathe contention and find it unfits me for serious work. My own belief is that we shall avoid a split but I *may* be forced to leave the League; but you may depend on it that

I will not do so till I am driven out of it. On the other hand it may become necessary for me to withdraw from the Council, and cultivate my own and other branches; in doing which hitherto I have had nothing but pleasant experiences and mostly helpful ones, too.

If any of the Branch are wishful to know my opinion and position further than they do know it, you are quite at liberty to show them this letter.

With best wishes to you and yours and greeting to all members of the Branch.

I am,
Yours very truly,
William Morris

This was followed by a letter written on the eve of the Socialist League Conference, in which Morris is in less uneasy mood about the outcome of it. He wants above all to get rid of two discordant policies being voiced by the League.

May 28, 1887.

My dear Glasse,

You see this is the crux: if the League passes a Parliamentary resolution the League, i.e., all members of it, are pledged to support that policy: but I think that policy is a mistake and cannot accept that pledge; if asked whether I agree with such a policy I must either answer no, or lie. This is no mere abstract difficulty, for during the past year Donald and others have been lecturing to branches (with mixed audiences at them of course) and have been preaching a policy which I and others have been attacking, to the great puzzlement of the lieges. What's to be done? We can't say yes and no to this question. I think the best way is for the differing individuals to join the differing bodies, and for those differing bodies to do each their own work without any hostility to each other: to work together wherever possible indeed, which can often be done.

I hate schism as much as you do, as all our people know well: indeed our parliamentary friends have been rather speculating on this knowledge; which I admit is more my fault than theirs; but now I must put my foot down. However, I don't think you need fear a split: a general negative to parliamentarianism will, I think, be carried, which will

84

not press on individuals unless they are on the Council. As to that body I think it would be far better for it not to have a "government and opposition", and to cease to trouble itself about anything but obvious business. Heaven knows we can find plenty of that to do. Keep up your spirits.

Yours ever,
William Morris

The last letter of the year 1887 opens with a reference to a hymn. Edward Carpenter, the writer of *England, Arise,* had appealed in a letter to *The Commonweal* (August 27th, 1887) for contributions toward a socialist song-book which he was preparing. John Glasse responded. A month later (October 22nd) *The Commonweal* printed *A Processional Hymn,* written by "J.G. of Edinburgh", to the tune *St. Gertrude* by Sir A. S. Sullivan. The rest of the letter is interesting not only for its remarks on Bernard Shaw[1] and the Fabians but also for yet another statement on the question of parliamentary action.

September 23, 1887.

My dear Glasse,

Many thanks for the hymn which is an acquisition. As to Sir A. Sullivan I don't know him, perhaps Carpenter himself might write to him: but I will find out if a friend or two that I know, may chance to know him.

As to *Commonweal* we will keep it up if possible: but of course it cannot be kept up at a weekly loss by a few donations: the whole body must help us to tide over the deficit and above all to *sell* the paper: the circulation *is* increasing however slowly, and I really think if we can keep it up for another year we shall have founded a self-supporting Socialist paper. As for "our differences", I feel nothing but conciliation about them: and in London I am sure that is the general feeling. As to what can be allowed, I don't think

1. Over half a century later Bernard Shaw (in a letter to Hesketh Pearson) wrote that "Morris knew by instinct that the Westminster parliament would sterilise the socialists, corrupt or seduce them, and change them from intransigent revolutionists into intriguers for Cabinet rank as Yesmen and bunk merchants in the service of the governing class, claiming all the time that they represented the interests of the proletariat. I was twenty-two years younger than Morris, and had not then gone into the history and nature of the Westminster Party system. . . ."

anyone ever proposed to interfere with the way in which private members might vote. But I don't see how any formal permission can be given to the branches to follow their own course of action (though I have no doubt they will do so). Because you see each branch ought to represent the general policy of the whole League being an integral and responsible part of it. However you may be sure that if the "parliamentary" section let the matter drop we shall not stir it; I can only hope that they will, and that our next Conference will concern itself wholly with means of propaganda and the support of *Commonweal*. I repeat that everybody up here belonging to the League are heartily sick of quarrelling. Perhaps that disreputable dog Aveling may try to stir up something though: and also there is a danger ahead in a kind of informal Conference now going on at Zurich, which I fancy has for its object an attack on the "Anarchists", i.e., all who will not swallow the German "Social Democrat" doctrines whole. I think that you will agree with me that this sort of pedantic tyranny must be resisted.

The attitude of Shaw also and his Fabians is rather difficult to get over: they are distinctly pushing forward that very useful association of lecturers as the only sound Socialist Body in the country: which I think is nonsense. For myself as I have told you before I have no wish to attack any body of Socialists: all I can say is that I would prefer to belong to a body that held aloof from parliamentary work, if such a body existed; and I think it very desirable, to say the least of it, that such a body should exist.

Of course, it's clearly no use talking of parliamentary action now: I admit, and always have admitted, that at some future period it may be necessary to use parliament mechanically: what I object to is *depending* on parliamentary agitation. There *must* be a great party, a great organisation outside parliament actively engaged in reconstructing society and learning administration whatever goes on in the parliament itself. This is in direct opposition to the view of the regular parliamentary section as represented by Shaw, who look upon parliament as *the* means; and it seems to me will fall into the error of moving earth and sea to fill the ballot boxes with Socialist votes which will not represent Socialist *men*. However, let them try it. I don't care so long as the League exists with the other aim of getting the workmen to look after their own affairs and thereby building up the new Society in the shell of the old one.

Excuse this long yarn.

With kindest regards and best wishes,

I am,

Yours fraternally,

William Morris

Soon after the last letter Morris produced (on 15th October, 1887) his socialist play *The Tables Turned, or Nupkins Awakened, a Socialist interlude*, for the benefit of *The Commonweal*. It was performed in the Socialist League headquarters in the Farringdon Road. Morris himself took the part of the Archbishop of Canterbury, a purse-proud and wooden-faced prelate. Bernard Shaw, who attended as a dramatic critic, witnessed it with delight and proclaimed Morris to be in the front rank of European playwrights. John Turner, founder of the Shop Assistants' Union (now merged in the Union of Shop, Distributive and Allied Workers) and for several years on the Trades Union Congress General Council from its formation in 1921, told me he had played a minor part in the performance. Like many actors of minor parts he remembered more than anything else the strong language used by the producer at the rehearsals and how fiercely Morris stamped and shouted when things went wrong. A. A. Purcell, who as Chairman of the Trades Union Congress in 1924 headed an official delegation (of which the same John Turner was a member) to the Soviet Union, also had vivid and somewhat similar recollections of the master-craftsman ("none better" he said) for whom he had worked at Merton Abbey. But, he said, he would never forget the day when Morris in a rage at bad workmanship threw the offender into a dyeing vat from which he emerged "a Green Man".

The great event, however, of the early winter of 1887 was "Bloody Sunday" in Trafalgar Square on 13th November: and to this in these letters Morris several times makes reference.

The right of public meeting in Trafalgar Square within

87

sight of the seats of government in Whitehall, which had been enjoyed for over a generation, was suddenly challenged by Sir Charles Warren, Commissioner of the Metropolitan Police. The ban imposed on such meetings was of doubtful legality: but in any case Londoners were not disposed to submit to it. A demonstration was organised. To disperse it the Home Office used an overwhelming force of policemen, infantry and cavalry. Blood was shed and the name of "Bloody Sunday" came to be attached to that November day.

For some weeks before that there had been a growing agitation on two issues, the coercion in Ireland, on which the Metropolitan Radical Association were making public protest, and the death sentences passed in Chicago on working-class agitators accused of incitement and violence. On this the Socialist League had supported the following resolution, "adopted at a meeting in South Place Chapel on 14th October, organised by Radical and Socialist bodies":

That the English workers in this meeting desire earnestly to urge on their fellow workers in America the great danger to public liberty that arises from suffering citizens to be punished for resisting attempts to suppress the rights of public meeting and free speech, since a right that the people are punished for enforcing is evidently thereby made no right at all, but a crime. That the fate of the seven men now under sentence of death for holding a public meeting in Chicago, at which certain policemen were killed for attempting forcibly to disperse the people and silence the speakers, is of deep concern to us as English workers, because their case is the case of Ireland today, and is likely to be ours tomorrow unless the workers from both sides of the Atlantic declare with one voice that all who interfere with the rights of public meeting act unlawfully and at their own peril. We cannot admit that the political views of the seven condemned men have anything to do with the principle involved; and we protest against their sentence, which, if carried out, will practically make the holding of meetings by working men in their own interests a capital offence throughout the United States of America, since it is

88

always possible for the authorities to provoke a crowd to reprisals involving danger to life.

At this point the Commissioner Sir Charles Warren,[1] had suddenly imposed his ban. Partly on the right of free speech and partly on the burning questions aforesaid, processions led by William Morris, John Burns, R. B. Cunninghame Graham and others marched to Trafalgar Square on Sunday, 13th November, 1887: and meantime the news had come that on the Friday the death sentences had been carried out in Chicago. In those days, however, it would be unlikely that any pressure from the United States Embassy could be the originating cause of suppression or brutality in Britain.

On that "Bloody Sunday", writes May Morris, onlookers saw "the extraordinary sight of citizens of London chased and driven by bodies of mounted police and squadrons of glittering Life Guards who charged round and round the Square scattering all who happened to be in their way". The scene was described and commented upon by Morris in the next week's *Commonweal* and by many others at the time and since. In the annual report of the Socialist League to its Conference six months later it is briefly related, and the statement is made:

> Two working men—Linnell and Curwen—met their death through the action of the police. The funerals of both these were attended by members of the Executive. The funeral of Linnell was made the occasion of probably the largest public demonstration ever held in London.

Morris spoke at Alfred Linnell's grave on 18th December: and wrote for that day the famous "Death Song". Three weeks later Morris wrote the following letter in which, after lecture arrangements and remarks on provincial organiser Mahon, he speaks of the League being in an eddy after the turbulence of the previous weeks.

1. Warren's resignation was accepted a year later, in November, 1888; it was occasioned, however, in connection with the "Jack the Ripper" murders.

My dear Glasse,

Many thanks for your letter and kind wishes which I reciprocate. As for my lecture for you, you may reckon on it, but I can give you no date just at present.

I intend to avail myself of my journey North to try a more extended lecture-tour in the N. generally: am prepared to spend a fortnight on it. This comes of a suggestion made to me that if I put myself into the hands of an agent he could arrange *paying* lectures for me in some places without which indeed I could not afford to do it. Of course I shall not make any charge to you or the Glasgow brethren. The time of this tour would depend a good deal on what you two sets of people thought the best time for up there: so you might write to Glasier and see what they think.

As to Mahon, I like him also, and when I last saw him had no doubt of his sincerity: but I think as I always thought that as things are the career of a professional agitator is not good for him, and I am afraid that he will do nothing else now. Also somehow he has (though a good natured fellow enough) a fatal gift of breeding squabbles, I scarcely know how. I suppose you know that the Glasgow chaps fairly quarrelled with him; of course I don't know all the story, but judge from a moderate account of it that I have had that he, knowing the turn of mind of our friends there, unnecessarily irritated them. When he was up in London he used to have "ideas" from time to time, which always ended in a quarrel. However he is still very young and if, as I hope, he is really "straight" he will no doubt better.

We are rather in an eddy here as far as the League is concerned; but I am not at all discouraged; for I think we can yet give a lift to it as an organisation; and, which is of more importance the general feeling is gaining ground much. The recent high handedness of the Government will do us good with the Radicals; and indeed it is coming to this that there is little difference between the ordinary uneducated Socialist and the Radical. This may be rather a slur on our followers, but it cannot be helped, and is after all the natural lines for the general movement in this country. Our own branch here is doing very well—which means simply that there are half a dozen energetic and painstaking men in it. Don't forget to do what you can for *Commonweal* up there. These winter months slacken off our sale and we are getting very hard up: and I suppose your sale falls off too.

Yours fraternally,
William Morris

The editor's anxiety about *The Commonweal* was warranted. In the fifty-two weeks to May, 1888, there were printed 163,500 copies, of which 152,186 were sold. There was a "gross loss" of about £270 which was partly met by donations of £188, leaving a net loss of a little over eighty pounds.

Meantime, arising from Trafalgar Square, a new organisation, the Law and Liberty League, was formed, consisting chiefly of radical and socialist bodies. "Your executive took no inconsiderable part in its formation and elected delegates, one of which (W. Morris) is a member of its executive", says the Report to the League's 4th Annual Conference. This, as well as a vexatious libel action (which, however, came to nothing), is touched on in the next letter.

February 10, 1888.

My dear Glasse,

Thanks for your note: I am trying to get the Glasgow people to get an invitation to me to give a lecture on art there, so that I may get part of my expenses paid; could the same thing be done in Edinburgh do you think? I should go down with a better conscience if I felt that the bourgeois were paying for my journey.

I may as well tell you that I am in somewhat of a mess. I am to have an action for libel brought against me for that article in the C. by one Reuss who is mentioned there and who was once a member of the S.L. I have no doubt myself of my facts, but proving them in a law Court is a different thing, and it will in any case bleed me seriously: hence my wish to spend as little as I can help on my nothern tour.

Also as I am not sure when the case is to come on my

dates *may* be interfered with. However I had better make them in spite of all that.

I am glad to hear that you have been doing well on the whole; the opinions are spreading fast, but for my part I can see nothing to be done *but* spreading the opinions: what we want is more intelligent men who can talk and argue on the matter.

This opening of Parliament is very discouraging to those who think much can be done at once. I really think that the Tories are firmer in their seat than I supposed even, some time ago. However there is no reason for discouragement for those who have always thought that the acceptance of the principles must be the first step: only the queer spasmodic action into which we are forced is very harassing to a quiet man like myself.

I suppose you saw that I am on the executive of the L.L.L. and in close alliance with Mrs. Besant and Stead. In short I have little life now outside the movement—which is as it should be.

Yours very truly,
William Morris

P.S.—I think I had better settle for March: some time after the 15th.

Burns and Cunninghame Graham were sentenced to six weeks' imprisonment for their share in Trafalgar Square ("unlawful assembly") and on 20th February, 1888, the Law and Liberty League celebrated their release with a meeting in Seymour Place Riding School. Michael Davitt was in the chair and among the speakers, including William O'Brien, W. T. Stead and Mrs. Besant, was also to have been Morris. But an "injudicious" speech by Hyndman brought an abrupt ending to the meeting, which was, says Morris, "very variously composed of Irish, Radicals and Socialists". To this meeting Morris refers:

February 20, 1888.

My dear Glasse,

Thank you for your note. I leave it entirely in your hands to make any arrangements you think favourable for me:

All I want is to be as little out of pocket as possible by the northern journey.

Will you kindly communicate with the Glasgow friends. I am now prepared to come on any date after the 20th March. I put it off till then because of the Commune Celebration in which this year we are going to join with the S.D.F. so I would not like to be absent, as that might be put down to hostility.

Events are rather stirring here again: our meeting of tonight is an important one since William O'Brien is coming; as it brings up London coercion into line with Irish. The Radicals too will be in good heart after the successes at Southwark and Edinburgh, and I think we shall make a mark.

Thanks for the Arbroath correspondence. I should think that such letters would do much good.

By the way, I have promised Mr. Forrest to lecture at Kilmarnock. Also I want to see an old friend now house-fast near Girvan in Ayrshire. These two visits must be taken into consideration by you and the Glasgow "bodies".

Yours fraternally,
William Morris

A rapid succession of letters follow, mainly about dates of speaking engagements—complexities for speakers which (like the boycott he mentions) have altered very little after seventy-five years.

February 28th, 1888

My dear Glasse,

Thanks for note: I am not quite sure that I can get away on the 21st as I am pledged to speak at the Commune Celebration, and owing to our being boycotted as to halls there is some doubt as to the day on which it will come off. So if the next week were feasible it might be better: but I may be able to be more certain after Thursday next. If I am not you had better settle for the later week though I should prefer the earlier. I will write on Friday as to the art lecture if the Edinburgh architects have such bad taste as not to be anxious to hear me. I think we had better not risk it. If the Edinburgh branch has a successful meeting &

can stand anything towards Commonweal, well & good. If not it can't be helped.

In haste,
Yours very truly,
William Morris

P.S. I have not heard from the Glasgow folk yet.

The experience of "Bloody Sunday" in Trafalgar Square was lodged firmly in his mind. A couple of years later Morris was able to build upon it in his *News from Nowhere* for an imaginative description of a crowd shot down by machine-guns, and so achieved a vision of what actually did happen thirty years afterwards not in Trafalgar Square but in Chillianwallah Bagh, commonly called the Amritsar Massacre.

March 2nd, 1888

My dear Glasse,

I am still unable to say whether I can get away on the 20th as I shall have to do if I am to speak at Kilmarnock or Glasgow on the 21st (you said Glasgow in your last). I have had no letter from Glasgow yet, & don't know what to do. I think I might make a week of it if I could have work found me: but it will be a great mistake to hurry it: I see then that the Glasgow Architect people like the Edinburgh ones don't like paying for me: this comes of my making myself too cheap: I shall never lecture gratis again except for a Socialist body, and I shall charge £20 & my expenses elsewhere.

I don't think the Glasgow people have chosen a good subject: who cares about history? I think I shall refuse to give it them. I think I might make Trafalgar Sq. the subject for the lecture at Edinburgh. I notice that out of London people are quite ignorant of the subject.

Yours very truly,
William Morris

Will write probably tomorrow.

POST CARD

March 14th, 1888

As to Girvan I did not intend staying more than one night there, but should like to get there earlyish one day

94

& not depart very early the next so as to get a few hours with my friend. I thought of leaving London on Tuesday night: so if Forrest has fixed for 23rd I might go to Girvan first: however I will wait till I hear from you.

Yours fraternally,
W. Morris

March 17, 1888

My dear Glasse,

I will go wherever I can be of use during my stay: only I have a letter from Glasier today asking me to make one at a gathering at Glasgow of Glasgow and Edinburgh friends which of course I should be glad to do if it can be managed, as I think a talk might be of service. Will you settle all this with Glasier and I shall be quite pleased with whatever you settle. As to the lectures I thought of giving: here they are. Art and Industry in the 14th Century (Glasgow) (only good for Glasgow or Edinburgh); Society of the future much the same; 3 Monopoly suitable anywhere; 4 What Socialists want, very elementary; 5 Socialism, an old old lecture, but would do where new to audience; 6 Socialism its end and methods: didn't I give this last year in Edinburgh? wants a rather advanced audience. I could also give half-hour's talk on Trafalgar Sq. and free speech, though I have no lecture.

Thanks for your invitation. I shall be very glad to see you—if I get to Edinburgh or indeed to Scotland at all. Whereof there seems some doubt in these snowy days: I look on it as quite an adventure putting myself on board a train. However I shall get there somehow I suppose.

Yours fraternally,
William Morris

Eighteen months elapse before the next letter. Just in this interval there were big developments both at home and abroad. Of these the most important was the convening in Paris for 14th July, 1889—the centenary of the storming of the Bastille that began the great French Revolution—of an "International Socialist Workingmen's Congress" in these words:

The Socialists of France could not permit the centenary of the bourgeois revolution to pass without asserting the close approach of a working-class revolution which, over the ruins of capitalist society, will proclaim equality for all men and women in the right to work, to the means of subsistence and to enjoyment.

But before it could be held one of the splinter parties of France called the "Possibilists" claimed sole right to organise such a Congress. Engels and the French socialists in touch with him found themselves compelled to bend every effort to deal with this schism. Engels had to lay aside for the time being his urgent work on the second and third volumes of *Capital.* It may be said, indeed, that just as Karl Marx was the moving spirit of the International Workingmen's Association (the First International) so Frederick Engels and the Marx family were the creator spirits that brought into being what came to be called "the Second International". They had to fight against opportunists and fainthearts and, in Britain, against the Social-Democratic Federation which supported the "Possibilist" Congress. The leaders of the bigger European parties followed the advice and promptings of Engels, and so did William Morris representing the Socialist League. When the summoning manifesto went out it was signed by names famous in the annals of European socialism: by Bebel and Liebknecht for Germany; Victor Adler for Austria; by Anseele for Belgium; by Domela Nieuwenhuis for Holland; by August Palm and Hjalmar Branting for Sweden; and in the case of Russia by Vera Zasulich, Plekhanov, Axelrod and Stepniak for the Union of Russian Social-Democrats. There were three organisations from Britain—the Socialist League, the Labour Association and the Ayrshire Miners' Union—the chief signatories for which were respectively William Morris; Cunninghame Graham, M.P., H. H. Champion and Tom Mann; and J. Keir Hardie. The summons went on to say:

Only the English Democratic Federation, setting itself in opposition to all the Socialist organisations which exist in Europe and America, has espoused the Possibilists' cause, without, however, claiming that its mere presence

96

will give an international character to a Possibilist congress so destitute of any international element.

Morris attended that Paris Congress out of which came the decision to set the 1st of May as the International Day of Labour. This accorded well with the outlook of Morris. The next year, in 1890, at Clerkenwell Green he headed a demonstration. In 1891 he spoke from one of the platforms in Hyde Park, and again in 1894. His poems and articles about May Day infused into it a revolutionary socialist content which has never been wholly lost.

At home also the "new unionism" had taken root, and the whole working-class movement was taking strides forward. In May, 1889, the Gas Workers' Union headed by Will Thorne came into being and won a strike in August. In August began the famous strike of the London Docks, led by John Burns, Tom Mann and Ben Tillett. In both of these Marx's daughter Eleanor was active. Morris realised its importance immediately ("the real point of the strike is the sense of combination which it is giving to the men"): and in the following letter the question comes up, along with a reference to the struggle of the "new unionists" against the old Lib.-Labs. in the Trades Union Congress.

September 9, 1889

My dear Glasse,

By all means use me as much as you can: I would not have thought of going to the Art Congress unless I had hoped to have been some use to our Scotch Comrades. I have a good lecture called the Origins of Ornamental Art which has a Socialist sting in his tail. I don't think I have delivered it at Edinburgh: I will give you that, and trust to impromptu (I am pretty good at it now) for my Socialist lecture if there is time for it. I hear that my Art Congress duties will not take more than three days, including a lecture "to the workmen" in the evening on some art-technical subject, e.g. dyeing. If the Glasgow people want me let us try to fit it in. I am writing to Glasier by this post.

As to the march of affairs the London strikes far outweigh

in importance the T.U. Congress. Of course we all know how conservative British workmen are: and I think the attack on Broadhurst went on wrong lines; he should have been attacked for his opinions and the actions resulting from them: I mean as being an obstructive and a Whig.

Thank you. I will accept with pleasure your invitation to come to your house. It is kind of you to keep me out of the hands of the Philistines. I hope however it will not inconvenience Mrs. Glasse.

Excuse haste. I am going out of town for a week and am much cluttered up with business.

Yours ever,
William Morris

It is clear from the recollections of May Morris (as also from these letters) how much Morris enjoyed staying at 16 Tantallon Place, with the Glasse family. Dr. Glasse himself had a fine voice and liked to sing old Scottish songs and ballads, not unexpectedly from one born in Auchtermuchty in "the kingdom of Fife". An Edinburgh correspondent, Mr. H. A. Scott, has given some further recollections about him, notably a meeting addressed by Hilaire Belloc on "The Socialist State" where Glasse from the chair "disassociated himself with some of Belloc's remarks".

The Art Congress mentioned in the letter of 9th September and then in the letters of October brings up yet another example of the stimulus Morris had given to the arts and of how he linked all up with socialist propaganda. Influenced by Morris a number of the younger men and women had organised an arts and crafts exhibition. This then resulted in the formation of the Arts and Crafts Exhibition Society of which one of the energetic organisers was Walter Crane, whose designs adorned socialist cards and journals three-quarters of a century ago. A second exhibition, to which Morris contributed both woven stuffs and printed cottons as well as the opening address (on Gothic architecture) in a course of lectures, was held that autumn of 1889 in the New Gallery in London. Meantime in Edinburgh an Art Congress was being organised under the ultra-respectable presidency of the

Marquis of Lorne. Glasse was keen to secure not only Morris but other speakers from amongst the visitors from London.

October 3rd, 1889

My dear Glasse,

As to date, the Congress opens on the 29th Oct., and I suppose I shall be on show for about 3 or 4 days: but I only have one night engagement as far as I know: for you had better in any case avoid any grand function for my date. I suppose I had better go to Glasgow after I have done with Edinburgh. Mr. Macartney[1] is the Sec. of our section:* he would tell you what are the dates of my evening engagements: however I will ask him as soon as I get back to town, as I am in the country at present. I would by all means ask Crane to speak for us: his address is Beaumont Lodge, Shepherds Bush. You might also get some work of T. Cobden Sanderson, Goodyers, Hendon, though that is more speculative. Dundee I cannot manage this time.

With best wishes,
Yours ever,
William Morris

* I suppose this address will find him.
National Association for the advancement of Art and its application to industry, 22, Albemarle St., London, W. [*Footnote by W.M.*]

In the next letter there is again mention of the "art-technical" lecture on dyeing which he had promised in September, 1889. The substance, if not the actual wording, of this lecture was published four years later in the volume edited by Walter Crane and entitled *Arts and Crafts Essays*. To this Morris wrote a preface, and contributed three essays, namely, *Of Dyeing as an Art, Textiles* and, with Emery Walker, *Printing*.

October 11th, 1889

My dear Glasse,

It seems that I am on on Wednesday and that after my address Crane reads a paper: which certainly would not be over till 4 as the Congress keeps up till 5 or past. Isn't it

1. Mervyn Macartney was to be architect to the Dean and Chapter of St. Paul's Cathedral, 1906–1931

doubtful in that case whether the afternoon would be a good time as it would compete with the Congress? let alone that Crane could not come on the Wednesday unless he could get his time. As for me of course I can do whatever you think best, remembering always that I am Congress engaged on *Wednesday* afternoon (not Tuesday: this has been altered) & Friday evening which same is the lecture on Dyeing to working men, as you might hint to our folk.

Excuse haste,

Yours ever,
W. Morris.

POST CARD

Oct. 12th, 1889

Dear G.,

My letter crossed yours, but to prevent mistake I repeat that Mr. Conway called on me on Thursday and told me that my special days were to be *Wednesday afternoon* and *Tuesday evening*. The former date of Tuesday afternoon having been changed. I leave you to do what you think best.

W. Morris

POST CARD

[postmarked October 16, 1889]

Dear G.,

All right I will be at your disposal on the Friday; will go to Glasgow; I have written to Crane about it also. Am coming on the Monday by the 10 a.m. train from Euston.

W.M.

Morris found the Art Congress "rather a dull job". Writing home about it he says:

Imagine one in the chair hour after hour listening to men teaching their grandmother to suck eggs, and I on my good behaviour too! I am very tired of it; but since the Tory evening paper here declares that Crane and I have spoiled the Congress, you may imagine we have not let all go by default. In point of fact, with the exception of Richmond, who gave a good address yesterday, there was nothing of any interest said except by Crane and me; and my lecture on dyeing to the workmen was really a success.

In more detail in his letter to his elder daughter (2nd November) he reports:

The Congress is now over, and Crane, Walker, Sanderson & myself go to Glasgow this afternoon. The Congress has not been much of a success, I fancy: I was in the chair at some monumentally dull papers; and you may imagine how I fidgetted, my dear. However I behaved pretty well and did my best to keep the dull times off them; apparently with some success, since the Dispatch, a Tory evening paper here, declares that the ill-success of the congress is owing to Crane and me and our Socialist vagaries: and in fact we managed to get a good deal of Socialism into our discourses. The Socialist meetings were quite successful. Walker after much suffering seems to have got through his lecture with credit. . . .

Immediately after leaving Scotland Morris was in Lancashire, Yorkshire and Derbyshire giving lectures, all of them carefully prepared and usually written out. For though he says in the next letter that he was "on the stump" Morris was incapable of treating an audience of working men with anything other than the best he could do.

November 21, 1889

My dear Glasse,

I am sending you a large paper copy of my new book (which I hope will not lumber your shelves too much) as a memento of the jolly week we had together.

I have been on the stump since at Liverpool, Chesterfield and Sheffield; and it seems to me as if the provinces were on the move; at Sheffield especially I had a large and enthusiastic audience. This is good since the movement cannot entirely live on London. Here I must say I think we are rather in an eddy, but I don't think it will last long.

Wishing you luck all round and plenty of encouraging work for the cause, and with kindest regards to Mrs. Glasse.

I am,
Yours fraternally,
William Morris

The reference to "my new book" was to *The Roots of the Mountains* which Morris had been writing throughout the year 1888 and which was published in November, 1889, with a special edition of 250 copies in quarto. Morris came to regard it as the best of his prose romances.

These romances, written in the last ten years of his life, have often been considered as something quite separate from his other work. Actually, throughout the 'eighties there is a close linkage between his activity and the romances. This is fairly obvious in the first of them as it appeared weekly in *The Commonweal* in 1886; all that Morris knew of English history and all that he had been learning from Marx's *Capital* are combined and flowering in *A Dream of John Ball*. But surely it should also have been clear that a peculiar aptitude in dealing with historical materialism would be shown by Morris who from boyhood had made the past his own,[1] who had respired from "every holt and heath" the past life of mankind on the earth and the deeds they had done. His Marxist studies in this field bore fruit in his next romance, *The House of the Wolfings*. This was published in December, 1888, and followed hard upon the publication in *The Commonweal*, from May, 1886, onwards, of the long series by Morris and Bax on *Socialism from the Root Up*.

But there was more to it than that. In *The Mark*, published in 1883, Frederick Engels had given a sketch of "primitive agrarian conditions" which all through the Middle Ages served as "the basis and as the type of all public institutions" and this "not only in Germany, but also in the north of France, England and Scandinavia". Its propagandist purpose was stated right away to be that "socialist working men, and through them the peasants, should learn" how the existing

1. In an autobiographical sketch of September, 1883, Morris wrote: "I went to school at Marlborough College, which was then a new and very rough school. As far as my school instruction went, I think I may fairly say I learned next to nothing there, for indeed next to nothing was taught; but the place is in a very beautiful country, thickly scattered over with prehistoric monuments, and I set myself eagerly to studying these and everything else that had any history in it, and so perhaps learned a good deal, especially as there was a good library at the school to which I sometimes had access."

system of landed property had arisen in contrast to "the old common property of all free men". It begins with "two fundamental facts" as governing primitive history: the grouping "according to kindred" and "common property" in the soil. Thus *The Mark* chimed in with all that Morris knew or had imagined.

On this there needs no argument: for the full title makes all clear: *A Tale of the House of the Wolfings and all the Kindreds of the Mark, written in prose and in verse by William Morris*. The technical terms then coming into use, endogamy and exogamy, matriarchy and patriarchy, totemic clans and all the rest, lurk unseen and unmentioned behind the vivid description of how Goths early fought against the aggressors of the Roman Empire. Instead we have one enlightening sentence:

> Also (to make an end at once of these matters of kinship and affinity) the men of one House might not wed the women of their own House: to the Wolfing men all Wolfing women were as sisters: they must needs wed with the Hartings or the Elkings or the Bearings, or other such Houses of the Mark as were not so close akin to the blood of the Wolf; and this was a law that none dreamed of breaking. Thus then dwelt this folk and such was their Custom.

So, too, it was with the next romance which tells how some centuries later another free Gothic people, now become dwellers in Burgdale, are able with their allies to withstand the murderous assaults of the Huns. This was *The Roots of the Mountains*.

Early in 1890 Morris, who had by that time received a "good word" from Glasse about the romance, is grateful for continued support but anxious about *The Commonweal*'s future. No longer editor (he was to be thrust out by the anarchist section now dominant, and domineering, within the Socialist League), Morris nevertheless contributes *News from Nowhere* serially in 1890 and does the best he can for the paper, until the long-expected break comes in November of that year.

February 17th, 1890

My dear Glasse,

I have already written to Mr. Morrison (not the brother) advising him by all means to steer clear of such a damnable business as "decoration". Of course he won't follow my advice, and then I shall be very happy to give any other advice as to details, most of which he will not be able to follow, but he is quite welcome to any of my barrenness. As to the article for Mr. Russell, I am so busy just now that I can promise nothing which involves *a date*. He had better write to me and give me particulars as to length & so on. I will get the last Christian Socialist & read your article, I am sure with pleasure.

Thank you for the good word about News from Nowhere: and also, and very specially, for that about the Roots: it gave me great pleasure to write it. I am glad you managed to shake off your blackguard, and that you are getting on well: please do what you can, you good folk to push the Weal we are in low water as to funds. I shall print the News from Nowhere in a book from 1/- or perhaps 6*d*.

Again thanks & best wishes.

Yours fraternally,
William Morris

Thereafter there is a gap of five years in the correspondence. Much happened in these five years. Quite apart from the foundation of the Kelmscott Press, the originality and significance of which[1] was brought out in the exhibition *The Typographical Adventure of William Morris* organised by the William Morris Society in 1957, there was the continuance of his other multifarious activities in Hammersmith and elsewhere. Communist writings were on a diminished scale (with no weekly paper making its insistent demands and with his health already impaired). Now came the prose romances. These no longer dealt directly (as did the first four of 1886 to 1890) with the same Marxist themes as he had been handling

1. In his Edinburgh lecture on "The Typographic Arts" in 1944 Stanley Morison, for many years foremost among European typographers, made reference to Morris as "one from whose life and example came a new and powerful and indeed permanent inspiration".

in weekly journalism and in agitation and propaganda up and down the country.

The skill of the artist was now expended on telling a story, for Morris was of the mould of Walter Scott or Homer in his power of story-telling. So there followed prose romances—which brought the fullest praise from the much-influenced W. B. Yeats, beginning with *The Story of the Glittering Plain* in 1891 and *The Wood Beyond the World* and culminating with *The Well at the World's End* on which he was busy at spare hours over several years. Posthumously printed were *The Water of the Wondrous Isles* and, partly unfinished, *The Sundering Flood*. Disdainfully regarded by modern critics—but not by poets—they are yet gems of literature and may one day be so acknowledged.

Of his communist writings and other activities of the 'nineties, a few only need be singled out, and those only from the one year—1893. That year had begun with the formation at Bradford of the Independent Labour Party. This led to a joint manifesto drawn up by William Morris for the Hammersmith Socialist Society, H. M. Hyndman for the Social-Democratic Federation, and Bernard Shaw for the Fabian Society. It was published on 1st May as *The Manifesto of English Socialists*.

The feeling for a united socialist party was now much in Morris's thoughts. Three months later he wrote to Emery Walker: "Whatever other people do, we the Hammersmith people must be careful to make as little quarrel with either party as we can help" (9th August, 1893). This sentiment comes out strongly in the conclusion of one of his lectures on communism to "the Hammersmith people" as follows:

Well, since our aim is so great and so much to be longed for, the substituting throughout all society of peace for war, pleasure and self-respect for grief and disgrace, we may well seek about strenuously for some means for starting our enterprise; and since it is just these means in which the difficulty lies, I appeal to all socialists, while they express their thoughts & feelings about them honestly and fearlessly, not to make a quarrel of it with those whose aim is one with theirs, because there is a difference of opinion between them about the usefulness of the details of the means. It is difficult or even impossible not to make mistakes about these, driven as we are by the swift lapse of time and the necessity for doing something amidst it all. So let us forgive the mistakes that others make, even if we make none ourselves, and be at peace amongst ourselves, that we may the better make War upon the monopolist.

["Communism"—lecture to Hammersmith Socialist Society (1893). Published and sold by the Fabian Society as Tract No. 113 in 1903]

It is in that lecture on communism that passages occur which have often been cited (partly because they were made readily available after Bernard Shaw had edited the lecture in 1903 as Fabian Tract No. 113) and may now be quoted again:

> For I do declare that any other state of society but communism is grievous & disgraceful to all belonging to it.

> Communism is in fact the completion of Socialism: when that ceases to be militant & becomes triumphant, it will be communism. The communist asserts in the first place that the resources of nature, mainly the land and those other things which can only be used for the reproduction of wealth and which are the effect of social work, should not be owned in severalty, but by the whole community for the benefit of the whole.

> Intelligence enough to conceive, courage enough to will, power enough to compel. If our ideas of a new Society are anything more than a dream, these three qualities must animate the due effective majority of the working-people; and then, I say, the thing will be done.

Morris, who had conducted some of his earliest agitation amongst workers in the coalfields, now championed their cause in the great lock-out of 1893. An autumn impulse from the mines, seen in the resistance of the colliers from the end of July to mid-November, brought from Morris a penetrating letter of support. After an opening paragraph it said:

Where is the bettering of condition for such indispensable workmen as the coal miners going to stop? Doubtless the gentlemen who live on their labour have asked themselves this question, and this lockout of their men has not been taken up only with a view to raising the price of coal (in which object they have been successful), but still more for the purpose of breaking down the power of the Miners' Federation, so that they (the owners) shall henceforth have the labour market wholly in their power. Most happily, it seems likely that in this latter aim they will be unsuccessful, in spite of the tremendous expenditure of their resources that the men have been driven into. The truth is that in this aim of establishing a grinding tyranny over the workers which shall be stable they are too late; the day is gone by for it.

The industrial tyranny of the individualist capitalist, masking itself under the guise of economic necessity, is bound to go the way of feudal tyranny appealing to the sanction of religion to justify itself.

The rallying conclusion was as follows:

I say, then, that we owe to the courageous and steadfast workmen who are now struggling in the interests of one and all a reward quite different from the semi-starvation which the gambling coal-owners would impose on them, and that to support them by all means in our power, pecuniary and otherwise, is a plain duty to all who are not pledged to the upholding the last and worst of the great tyrannies of the world, the plutocratic, to wit.

[*The Sun*, 16th October, 1893]

Other socialist or communist concerns went on steadily in the 'nineties: and it was to one of a convivial nature that the poet invited Glasse who was on a visit to London. On this occasion Dr. Glasse met Sydney Cockerell, then Morris's secretary, who was in his late twenties. He was to keep the memory of Morris undimmed for over sixty-five years till his death in 1962. The letter of invitation ran:

March 11th, 1895

My dear Glasse,

I shall be very pleased to see you on Wednesday: only I may have to go to the Socialist Supper Club to dinner, as I have been remiss in attendance of late. In that case I propose to take you with me as a guest, as they will be very glad to see you. In case, come not later than, say, 6 p.m. and then if you don't like to go, we will stay at home.

Yours very truly,
William Morris

Seven months later, on 13th October, 1895, Sidney Webb was billed for a Sunday-evening lecture to the Hammersmith Socialist Society and was there suitably entertained. Many years afterwards, when asked by the present writer what had been Morris's comment, Webb replied that Morris had said to him as they parted: "The world is going your way at present, Webb, but it is not the right way in the end."

CHAPTER SIX

MORRIS'S REVOLUTIONARY WRITINGS

THE revolutionary socialist writings or, as we may now call them, the communist writings of William Morris, are to be found chiefly in *The Commonweal* (1885–90) and other socialist journals. In *The Commonweal* he poured forth editorial articles, political notes, serial articles (several reprinted afterwards as pamphlets or in book form), dialogues, old stories retold, such as the *Revolt of Ghent*, short occasional poems, one long serial poem, *The Pilgrims of Hope*, and serial stories such as *A Dream of John Ball* and *News from Nowhere*.

But anyone who seeks to find Morris's standpoint on war, on the colonial question, on the monarchy, etc., etc., as revealed in his current comments (the liveliest vehicle of man's thoughts), will look in vain in the Collected Edition published in 1910–15. For the principle followed in these twenty-four thick quarto volumes was to exclude much that did not appear to the publishers to possess "literary merit". At any rate this was the explanation furnished by the publishers (that they did not wish to publish anything "beneath the dignity" of the poet's reputation) in a letter to the late Joan Tuckett, who, herself a talented theatrical producer, had asked why Morris's socialist play was not made available in a reprint. This play, *The Tables Turned, or Nupkins Awakened, a Socialist interlude*, was thus quietly dropped out of the canon of Morris's writings.

The Collected Edition, taking up over a yard of bookshelf, had been edited by his younger daughter, May Morris, who tried in other ways also to keep her father's memory green, and even to carry on his work as opportunity offered. When it seemed to her, in the post-war year 1919, that Britain was nearing a revolutionary situation she helped to found the

Kelmscott Fellowship, some of whose members, and prominent amongst them J. L. Mahon, brought out a special number of the old *Commonweal*. Not content with the incomplete edition, the indomitable[1] May Morris bided her time; and twenty years after, at the centenary wave-crest of her father's renown, gladly accepted the proffered help of Sir Basil Blackwell. Hence the magnificent pair of supplementary volumes, published by him in 1936.

Apart from what had been reprinted from *The Commonweal* at the time, or later, the political notes and editorial articles in it by Morris are dismissed by J. W. Mackail, his chief biographer, with the bookish man's lofty contempt: "There is little to say except that he, no more than other men, escaped the vices of journalism when he took to being a journalist."

Now when Mackail took to being a biographer there was little to say except that he, no more than other men, escaped the vices of biography. Yet these were not so much positive vices as defects which might have escaped notice to the present day (except perhaps amongst those whose political affiliation would make them treasure Morris's communist comment on current affairs in the 'eighties) but for the fact that a friend of Morris was able to review *The Life of William Morris* on its appearance in 1899. This was Bernard Shaw, who exactly fifty years later was able to recall that Mackail looked upon Morris's communism "as a deplorable aberration, and even in my presence was unable to quite conceal his opinion of me as Morris's most undesirable associate. From his point of view Morris took to Socialism as Poe took to drink."[2] Similarly in his 1899 review, Shaw showed, while

1. Once at Kelmscott Manor, where the writer was discussing with May Morris its future custody, she referred suddenly to the other William Morris (the motor multi-millionaire, then a supporter of the Blackshirts) and said explosively: "This Lord Nuffield, with all his money—not *his* money, but money that he stole from the workers." Clearly, a chip of the old block.

2. *Observer*, 6th November, 1949. Two weeks later in *The Observer* Sir Sydney Cockerell, who had that year written a preface to a re-issue of Mackail's book, wrote a letter in which he sought to controvert Shaw's suggestion.

acknowledging the excellence of the book, that Mackail was aloof and unconsciously disdainful of Morris's activities. For example: "Fortunately for himself, Mr. Mackail knows little more about this part of Morris's life than might be gathered by any stranger from the available documents."

Morris in the book is shown "as going through a certain curriculum of lectures and propaganda, like a man who takes up a subject and works his way through it much as a university student does, except in a rather eccentric and ungentlemanly way, and in a perhaps rather shady set". The biography sometimes "treats the street corner exploits on which Morris rightly valued himself with an indulgence which implies that Mr. Mackail regards them as slightly vulgar follies. . . . In fact, not being interested himself in this part of his work, he does not make it very interesting to others, and makes Morris's Socialism produce, on the whole, the effect of a mere aberration." On the contrary, as Shaw put it, in 1936, with an insight that had grown greater with the years, "Morris's writings about Socialism, which the most uppish of his friends regarded as a deplorable waste of the time and genius of a great artist, really called up all his mental reserves for the first time."

Actually, it is in some of these current "journalistic", "ephemeral" comments and notes in *The Commonweal* that the man comes alive as much as anywhere. One of the best ways to gain a picture of the workers' struggle in the 'eighties, of the doings of the socialists and of Morris's own revolutionary activities, is to turn over the pages of *The Commonweal*.

Take the year 1887 at a venture. Open the first number, published on 1st January, and on the first page the war-danger then threatening is dealt with by Morris in these words:

> Meanwhile if war really becomes imminent our duties as Socialists are clear enough, and do not differ from those we have to act on ordinarily. To further the spread of international feeling between the workers by all means possible; to point out to our own workmen that foreign competition and rivalry, or commercial war, culminating

at last in open war, are necessities of the plundering classes; and that the race and commercial quarrels of these classes only concern us so far as we can use them as opportunities for fostering discontent and revolution; that the interests of the workmen are the same in all countries and they can never be really enemies of each other.

"*Opportunities for fostering discontent and revolution.*" It is twenty years later that the 7th International Socialist Congress at Stuttgart passes the famous resolution for the prevention of war, with its final clause:

Should war break out, it is their duty [i.e. the duty of the workers and their Socialist leaders] to intervene for its speedy ending and with all their powers to use the economic and political crisis created by the war to rouse the masses and thereby to hasten the overthrow of capitalist rule.

It is thirty years later that Lenin, fighting stubbornly against all those leaders of the Socialist International who abruptly changed over in a week from being pacifists into becoming warmongers and recruiting sergeants, carries through the international socialist decision, deepens and sharpens the struggle, and thereby hastens effectively and indeed leads the workers in bringing about the "overthrow of capitalist rule". Surely this thirty-year-old thought of William Morris would not have seemed just "one of the vices of journalism" amid the war crises of 1914 onwards.

If, however, anyone would suggest that Morris was simply a pacifist or a Tolstoyan in his attitude, let them turn to the article written to celebrate the men of the Commune of Paris— ("We honour them", says Morris, "as the foundation stone of the new world that is to be")—and read how he bids his readers think that it would be "well for them to take part in such an armed struggle within Britain".

"Remember", he says in another place, "that the body of people who have, for instance, ruined India, starved and gagged Ireland, and tortured Egypt, have capacities in them

—some ominous signs of which they have lately shown—for *openly* playing the tyrant's game nearer home."

To linger over the pages of *The Commonweal* to recover those buried thoughts of the 'eighties is tempting: but we may take leave of it with one last citation. When modern socialists hasten to defend the British monarchy; when so many, too, of Morris's old associates had taken knighthoods from "the Fountain of Honour", it is refreshing to quote Morris's own attitude on the monarch of the day, who was not to be given the gratification of snubbing her Liberal ministers for nominating Morris Poet Laureate.[1] "What a nuisance", he says, "the monarchy and court can be as a centre of hypocrisy and corruption, and the densest form of stupidity." The Jubilee of Queen Victoria is for Morris "hideous, revolting and vulgar tomfoolery". "One's indignation", he writes, "swells pretty much to the bursting point." The "great Queen", Victoria, for him was a representative of capitalism; and her life was that of "a respectable officer, who has always been careful to give the minimum of work for the maximum of pay". In the very height of the loyalist orgy, to-day paralleled by the vamped-up excitement of royal weddings and parturitions, Morris dismisses "this loathsome subject of the Jubilee" with the hope that it "may deepen the discontent a little . . . when people wake up as on the morning of a disgraceful orgy".

When we turn from these least-known writings of Morris to his best-known writings—the serial stories in *The Commonweal*—it might seem that these, in their wide circulation, would have killed the Morris-myth. Anyone who thinks so does not realise how persistent and all-pervading has been the anti-Marxist propaganda around the name and fame of Morris, does not remember that "the lie is a European power".

Take *News from Nowhere: Or an Epoch of Rest, being some Chapters from a Utopian Romance*, which has gone through

1. Morris, a few years later, on the death of Lord Tennyson, was "sounded" by the Cabinet as to whether he would take the Poet Laureateship if offered. Morris declined.

many reprints and is his best-known work.[1] It was translated into German by Marx's old friend Liebknecht and was circulating in Russia for years before the revolution. Yet, in the case of this book, the poison ivy of the myth has completely hidden the oak. Almost everyone appears to have read *News from Nowhere* under the domination of the Morris-myth and have, in consequence, read not what was in the book but what they expected to find there.

The essence of the presentation of the change from the old society to the new in *News from Nowhere* is through the development of revolutionary class struggle up to the establishment of working-class power.[2] In the tale, the workers at last learn "how to combine" and, with betterment of their conditions "forced from the masters", get so far that there is alarm in the master class, and novel steps have to be taken. In passages of almost uncanny insight Morris tells how a "mixed economy" brought about by the reformists ("the State Socialists") ended in muddle. Then comes a further development of class struggle, a period of vast unemployment, strikes and demonstrations met by repression and armed force leading to a successful General Strike; after which the counter-revolutionary measures by the most reactionary sections were defeated by the working class, concentrated in militant struggle against the capitalist class. When in the end it reaches the stage of civil war, "the greater part, certainly the best part, of the soldiers joined the side of the people" and the issue was not long in doubt.

Thirty years later it took all the force of Lenin's genius

1. For many years I made it a practice to ask three questions, which were almost invariably answered as follows:
Question 1: Have you read *News from Nowhere*?
Answer: Yes, a long time ago.
Question 2: What would you say about it?
Answer: A beautiful dream of a future society, but quite impossible.
Question 3: Do you remember how the change took place to the future society?
Answer: No, I can't say that I do remember.

2. It calls to mind Marx's letter to Weydemeyer of 5th March, 1852, where Marx says "the class struggle necessarily leads to the *dictatorship of the proletariat*" and "this dictatorship itself only constitutes the transition to the *abolition of all classes* and to a *classless society*".

114

and profound knowledge of Marxism to restore in a revolutionary epoch the actual teachings of Marx and Engels.

The vindication of this teaching was shown in the victory of the Russian Revolution; the defeat of the wars of intervention and of fascist counter-revolution and the extension of communism in Europe and Asia with the further victories of the Chinese Revolution in 1949 and the Cuban Revolution in 1959.

The fact that these victories have brought such a transformation in the balance of the world situation that the possibility has now arisen in given concrete conditions in given countries for a peaceful transition to socialism, is not a refutation of these teachings of Marx and Lenin, or of the picture presented by Morris, but rather a vindication of their triumphant outcome.[1]

The vulgarity of the Morris-myth appears particularly in its treatment of Morris, who had written these romances, as thereby belonging to the school of Utopian Socialism—which, as a Marxist, he so explicit and strongly condemned. See especially his painstaking analysis of the chief Utopian Socialists in *Socialism: Its Growth and Outcome*. One chapter of it ("The Utopists: Owen, Saint Simon, and Fourier") deals with the school of thinkers who preceded the birth of "modern scientific or revolutionary Socialism" and says:

> These men thought it possible to regenerate Society by laying before it its shortcomings, follies, and injustice, and by teaching through precept and example certain schemes of reconstruction built up from the aspirations and insight of the teachers themselves. They had not learned to recognise the sequence of events that *forces* social changes on mankind whether they are conscious of its force or not . . . They hoped to convert people to Socialism, to accepting it consciously and formally, by showing them the contrast

1. "To-day, in a number of capitalist countries the working class, headed by its vanguard, has the opportunity, given a united working class and popular front or other workable forms of agreement and political co-operation between the different parties and public organisation, to unite a majority of the people, win state power without civil war and ensure the transfer of the basic means of production to the hands of the people." (*Declaration of 81 Communist Parties in 1960*)

between the confusion and misery of civilisation, and the order and happiness of the world which they foresaw. From the elaborate and detailed schemes of future Society which they built up they have been called the Utopists.

Then, of the various communities which owed their origin to Utopian Socialism, it is said clearly and bluntly that:

> Their conditions of life have no claim to the title of Communism, which most unluckily has often been applied to them. Communism can never be realised till the present system of Society has been destroyed by the workers taking hold of the political power. When that happens, it will mean that Communism is on the point of absorbing and transmuting Civilisation all the world over.

In the late 'eighties Edward Bellamy, a citizen of Boston, Massachusetts, wrote *Looking Backward* (that is, from the year A.D. 2000) and the book ran into several editions. *Looking Backward* described a socialist society which had developed without class struggle out of the growth of bigger and bigger monopolies until there was only one monopoly—which would include the whole people. Morris, who could not abide this "cockneyfied paradise", made a kindly enough but extremely searching criticism of the book in *The Commonweal* in June, 1889, saying:

> The only ideal of life which such a man can see is that of the industrious *professional* middle-class men of to-day purified from their crime of complicity with the monopolist class, and become independent instead of being, as they now are, parasitical.

Once Morris had published his review of the Bostonian's Utopia, he had, like all critics, set himself a challenge. This challenge he met magnificently six months later when he began to publish *News from Nowhere* as his "chapters from a Utopian romance", showing how the thing should be done and laying stress not on machinery but on the relations of man to man.

Morris set out in *News from Nowhere* to write a Utopian romance about a communist society, about what Marx called the "higher phase" of communism. A romance is not to be judged like a treatise, and clearly some of the matters in *News from Nowhere* are set down by Morris just as they came to his mind. Yet much in it answers to the indications given by Marx in his notes on the "Gotha Programme"[1]. It even anticipated some of the features already beginning to show themselves in embryo as soon as the first Five-Year Plan in the Union of Soviet Socialist Republics had laid the material basis for socialism.

Those who failed to see the insistence upon the proletarian class struggle as a central feature of *News from Nowhere* also blamed Morris, because, unlike Anatole France, in his *White Stone*, he did not draw a picture of the marvellous machinery of the future society. But since it is precisely the same type of people who omitted to note, in the case of Anatole France, the insistence on the proletarian dictatorship as a preliminary to his future society—and this in a book written ten years before the Russian Revolution—their views of Morris can have but little value. Supposing Morris had made his book hum with machines and complicated metal devices, what would have happened? Such machines, imagined before the age of X-rays or radio-activity, of automobiles or flying machines, of wireless waves or television, would have been not the machines of a communist society, but of a decade, or at most, of two decades, ahead of 1890. Morris did not care to display the wooden imagination of an H. G. Wells in his *Anticipations*, which would have made his book take on the peculiarly ephemeral quality of Wells's early twentieth-century writings. Thus Morris, while missing the local popularity of the man who can tell what the parson is going to have

1. "In a higher phase of communist society, after the enslaving subordination of individuals under division of labour, and therewith also the antithesis between mental and physical labour, has vanished; after labour, from a mere means of life, has itself become the prime necessity of life; after the productive forces have also increased with the all-round development of the individual, and all the springs of co-operative wealth flow more abundantly—only then can the narrow horizon of bourgeois right be fully left behind and society inscribe on its banners: 'from each according to his ability, to each according to his needs!' " (*Critique of the Gotha Programme*)

for dinner by virtue of having peeped over the vicarage wall and seen the cook plucking the mint, did work of a more lasting value. What Morris says is that the productive forces have enormously developed in communist society. "The great change in *the use of mechanical force*" which he mentions was the basis of his conception of work ceasing to be useless toil and becoming a healthy need like play. As for the new power and the actual machines, he says simply that they were beyond his comprehension or capacity to explain.

For Morris was not concerned simply with the improved and novel machinery which he assumed as the basis of heavy industry and transportation, but with the relations of men in the process of production. Given these developed productive powers, his business was to imagine a world with no exploitation of man by man, with no birthmarks of capitalism, or—to give it a local habitation and a name—to picture the lower and upper reaches of the Thames as they would be in the higher phase of communism.

Morris goes on to make one assumption, which is unlikely enough, namely, that after the material basis of communism is laid there comes to mankind an epoch of rest wherein men express their joy in labour largely through handicraft. Nevertheless, this assumption of a temporary epoch of rest before the advance of mankind to further heights of communist development is an essential part of Morris's picture. Once this assumption was made, what else was to be expected but that Morris would hark back to the London as it once was, where "Geoffrey Chaucer's pen moves over bills of lading", to get some concrete idea of what it again might be. So the stones of his buildings seem hewn out of the masonry of the Middle Ages, and the picture recalls the opening lines of his *Earthly Paradise*:

> Forget six counties overhung with smoke,
> Forget the snorting steam and piston stroke,
> Forget the spreading of the hideous town;
> Think rather of the pack-horse on the down,
> And dream of London, small and white and clean,
> The clear Thames bordered by its gardens green.

There is a prevalent objection to the absorption of Morris in the Middle Ages, partly due to the myth-mongers, and also in part due to the lack of understanding of Utopias and how they are made and imagined. After the Renaissance Utopias of Sir Thomas More and Rabelais, the first great outburst of Utopian thoughts and imagination was in the writings of the French revolutionaries, who imagined "justice", "equality" and all other "republican virtues" to be just round the corner. But when they wanted symbols of their dreams they evoked the ancient republics of Rome and Sparta, the toga and the Phrygian cap. Utopians all look back to a golden age and then project it into the future.

If the ancient world of the slave-holders may be used in a transfigured form by other writers, then William Morris may evoke John Ball instead of Spartacus, or Chaucer's London instead of Lacedaemon. So presently, in this romance, some of the atmosphere of the transfigured Middle Ages is built up as the antithesis to the atmosphere of London seventy years ago. But this atmosphere, this fragrance of the Garden of England wherein this communist dialogue is held, so overpoweringly assails the senses already drugged by the pervading myth that, seemingly, many who wander there hear the *News from Nowhere* but do not hearken to it; remember the fragrance of the garden, but nothing of the men who dwell therein. It is as though readers of the Dialogues of Plato were to remember only their setting—the shady plane tree beyond the banks of the Cephisos and Socrates paddling his feet in the burn—but forget what the Dialogue was about.

We, who can look back over the developing years since Morris wrote, can see with what insight he beheld the class struggle in Europe. Had he lived another ten years he would have seen many features of his chapter on "How the Change Came" enacted in the year 1905 in Russia, from the January massacre in St. Petersburg, through the mutinies of the armed forces and the General Strike to the creation of Soviets ("Workers' Committees", Morris called them), the formation of the Black Hundreds (the "Friends of Order", Morris called them), and finally the armed rising.

Again, the growth of fascist gangs in Britain in the 'twenties and 'thirties is evidence of the poet's foresight; in *News from Nowhere* old Hammond in A.D. 2112 tells the story of what happened.

> A great part of the upper and middle classes were determined to set on foot a counter-revolution; for the Communism which now loomed ahead seemed quite unendurable to them. Bands of young men, like the marauders in the great strike of whom I told you just now, armed themselves and drilled, and began on any opportunity or pretence to skirmish with the people in the streets. The Government neither helped them nor put them down, but stood by, hoping that something might come of it. These "Friends of Order", as they were called, had some successes at first, and grew bolder.
>
> A sort of irregular war was carried on with varied success all over the country; and at last the Government, which at first pretended to ignore the struggle, or treat it as mere rioting, definitely declared for "the Friends of Order".[1]

It can be seen with what insight Morris could pierce the veil of the future, with what skill he was able to "state the case" for communism and also to show how the struggle of the working class was the only means to lead the whole people to that final aim. In different circumstances, but still in the same country, *The British Road to Socialism* claims to show to a later generation not only the way forward but the aim worked out in detail.

Britain is a country where the older political parties hark back many a generation for their political progenitors, the Tories to Burke and Bolingbroke, the Liberals to Cromwell and Charles James Fox. It is not so with the younger parties. The Labour Party occasionally goes out of its way to claim Marx and Engels (and more often disclaims them) while Morris (usually in the trappings of the Menshevik-myth) is

1. The *Fascist Weekly* at the time of the Morris Centenary had the impudence to claim him as a forerunner of fascism on the ground that he was "imbued with the Viking spirit". This was "canonisation" with a vengeance!

now and again called upon for sentences or lines to garnish a platform oration: but no more than that. The Communist Party, on the other hand, while insistently claiming Marx and Engels as guides to action (as do also eighty other Communist parties), makes a special claim of affiliation to William Morris. In a London conference held in May, 1948, "under the auspices of the National Cultural Committee of the Communist Party", this affiliation was stressed by Professor George Thomson (speaking on "Our National Cultural Heritage") who was followed by architects and painters, authors like Jack Lindsay and Andrew Rothstein, and others, nearly all of whom (apart from J. D. Bernal, F.R.S., on "Britain's Heritage of Science") followed on the same subject until the historian A. L. Morton could say: "William Morris, whose name has so rightly run through our Conference like a red thread, taught us one thing above all: that it is not work which is the curse, but servile, joyless work in which the man becomes a hand."

A Dream of John Ball has also suffered from the myth-makers. It is highly praised as a dream of beauty, as a vessel of wonderful thoughts on mankind and its destiny, as a work of artistic perfection; and amid these generalities of praise for its form the revolutionary content is forgotten.

Certainly it is a wonderful piece of work. The revolutionary socialist falls asleep and dreams; and in his dream awakens on a highway in Kent in the year of the Peasants' Revolt (for in 1381 the peasants overthrew their lords, came to London, captured it and executed the Archbishop of Canterbury). Then he hears an agitator of the time, John Ball, just released by the rebels from the Archbishop's prison, stand up and exhort the armed peasants in words that have the double quality of heartening the workers in their struggle to-day, as well as of summoning to life the struggle of the oppressed five centuries and more agone.

Forsooth, in the belly of every rich man dwelleth a devil of hell, and when the man would give his goods to the poor, the devil within him gainsayeth it, and saith, "Wilt thou then be of the poor, and suffer cold and hunger and mocking as they suffer, then give thou thy goods to them, and keep them not." And when he would be compassionate, again saith the devil to him, "If thou heed these losels and turn on them a face like to their faces, and deem of them as men, then shall they scorn thee, and evil shall come of it, and even one day they shall fall on thee to slay thee when they have learned that thou art but as they be."

And how shall it be then when these are gone? What else shall ye lack when ye lack masters? Ye shall not lack for the fields ye have tilled, nor the houses ye have built, nor the cloth ye have woven; all these shall be yours, and whatso ye will of all that the earth beareth; then shall no man mow the deep grass for another, while his own kine lack cow-meat; and he that soweth shall reap, and the reaper shall eat in fellowship the harvest that in fellowship he hath won; and he that buildeth a house shall dwell in it with those that he biddeth of his free will; and the tithe barn shall garner the wheat for all men to eat of when the seasons are untoward, and the rain-drift hideth the sheaves in August; and all shall be without money and without price.

Some seventy pages long it is, and in this short compass the great opening sentence of the *Communist Manifesto* of 1848, "the history of all human society, past and present, has been the history of class struggles", is illustrated from the climax in England of the struggle between baron and serf.

Then a marvellous change takes place in the story, marvellous in that without any clumsiness or any sense of anachronism the dreamer and John Ball begin to talk of the days to come and in this talk five hundred years or more of the future are unrolled. In the language of the greatest simplicity and beauty the beginnings of capitalism, its primitive accumulation, its driving of the peasants from the land and the formation of a class of "free labourers", its enormous heaping up of wares of all kinds, its extraction of surplus value, its development into cyclical crises, its trickery of capitalist democracy and its final defeat by the workers are foretold. Morris had been studying the first volume of Marx's

Capital with some care, had been arguing out all the analyses of capitalist society with his associates in the Socialist League; and those who are curious may trace how the chapter headings of *Capital* run like themes through this part of the vision, and are ever reinforced by the faith in the struggle of the workers and their ultimate victory. Everything that Morris knew of the Middle Ages—and that was more than any other artist of his time—combines with all his experience of work and struggle and all his learning of Marxism to make one of the great imaginative books of the world, as true to life as the most painstaking scientific research[1] and itself alive.

In all Morris's writing during his great period, the poet has become the revolutionary fighter whose special skill, energies and insight are devoted to the class struggle. *A Dream of John Ball* is revolutionary. *A King's Lesson*—that marvellous picture of the life of the lord and the serf—is a revolutionary lesson. The poems he wrote were chants for socialists who were then revolutionaries; or, as in his larger unfinished poem, *The Pilgrims of Hope*, devoted to the life of a proletarian and the struggles of the workers, culminating in the Paris Commune. If Morris, the "implacable enemy" of Victorian civilisation, could be deemed by Bernard Shaw to have been "the greatest poet, the greatest prose writer and the greatest craftsman of the reign", then surely it may be said, not only of his poetry, but of all his manifold genius, of his whole high power of communication in prose and verse, that it had been turned by Morris into a revolutionary weapon.

1. A tribute to "William Morris's unforgettable picture" (of the dinner in the harvest field) in Part II of *The Earthly Paradise* was paid in *The Medieval Village* (1926) by G. G. Coulton who wrote in 1934 to say: "I still think his *The Man born to be King* one of the most (if not *the* most) Chaucerian of narrative poems."

A NOTE ON BOOKS AND SOCIETIES

WILLIAM MORRIS was publishing his poems and other writings only for a short forty years. Even so, they fill the two dozen volumes which his devoted daughter edited fifty years ago, followed by two supplementary volumes. The whole of his books, themselves only a small part of his artistic activities, were listed in a bibliography by H. Buxton Forman in the middle 'nineties, and also in Aylmer Vallance's *William Morris*, the appendices to which list not only the printed works but also (up to 1898) the publications of the Kelmscott Press: and for these last there is, of course, the annotated list given by S. C. Cockerell in 1898 together with the note by William Morris on his aims in founding the Press.

His life and times were dealt with in fairly full detail first by the official or Burne-Jones family biography entrusted to Lady Georgiana's son-in-law, the Latin scholar and Board of Education inspector, J. W. Mackail. This, published in 1899, was reprinted in the series of "World Classics" with an introduction by Sir Sydney Cockerell in 1950. It had been the subject of caustic comment by Bernard Shaw when it first appeared for its mimimising of the socialist or communist activities of Morris. Secondly, his later life and times, especially the detail of the socialist movement, were recalled somewhat diffusely but in loving detail by May Morris in each of the twenty-four volumes, the impact of which was somewhat diminished by the war raging at the time its publication was completed.

In the last sixty years the number of books about Morris have been legion, and almost certainly amount to more pages than have been devoted in the same period to Browning or

Swinburne or Tennyson or any other of his coevals in the reign of Victoria.

A full bibliography of all these books on Morris, poor stuff though some of them may be, as well as of publications in other languages was, therefore, long overdue. The gap has at last been filled by an American scholar, Professor E. D. Le Mire, to whose edition of ten unpublished lectures of Morris is appended a 200-page bibliography. This work, at present available only on microfilm, is shortly to be published. *The Journal of the William Morris Society* publishes an annual bibliography of books on Morris.

There is also a need for a chronicle of the life of Morris, showing where he was each day or week and what he was making or doing. The Victoria and Albert Museum, South Kensington, which owed so much to the fostering care and help bestowed on it by William Morris, would be the obvious official body to measure up to this and assign members of its skilled staff for the purpose, were it not that the niggard and philistine parsimony of successive British governments towards museums and libraries would almost certainly put it out of the question. As it is, members of the various voluntary organisations that stem from William Morris will probably have to undertake this task.

Against the persistence of the Morris-myth for several generations a counter-current set in about a third of a century ago. In parliamentary backwaters, however, the Menshevik-myth could still be found as late as January, 1948, when there was a brisk interchange between Prime Minister Attlee and William Gallacher, parliamentary leader of the Communist Party. The latter had said that: "The Communist ideology was there in the writings, speeches and poems of the great artist and poet, William Morris, long before there was a Soviet Russia." The Prime Minister, who in an earlier debate had startled his fellow public-school boys by an erroneous declaration that there never had been a third Punic War, now confessed himself "amazed at the effrontery of the Hon. Member for West Fife in appealing to the memory" of Morris. "William Morris," he went on to declare, "was the last man in the world who would ever have bowed to any Marxian authority."

The counter-current owed much to the books that follow:

William Morris: Artist Writer Socialist by May Morris. Volume II. *Morris as a Socialist* with an account of *William Morris as I knew him* by Bernard Shaw. Oxford: Basil Blackwell. 1936.

The Letters of William Morris to his Family and Friends. Edited by Philip Henderson. Longmans, Green and Company. 1950.

William Morris: Romantic to Revolutionary by E. P. Thompson. Lawrence and Wishart Ltd. 1955.

In addition, amongst the many anthologies, some in verse and some, especially latterly, in prose, the following may be singled out:

William Morris: Selected Writings. Edited with an introduction by G. D. H. Cole for the Nonesuch Press, Bloomsbury. 1934.

William Morris: Selected Writings and Designs. Edited, with an introduction by Asa Briggs. With a supplement by Graeme Shankland on William Morris, Designer. Illustrated by twenty-four plates. Published by Penguin Books. 1962.

William Morris: Victoria and Albert Museum picture book. Published by H.M.S.O. 1958.

Catalogue of an Exhibition of Victorian and Edwardian Dramatic Arts at the Victoria and Albert Museum, H.M.S.O. 1952.

Catalogue of the William Morris Gallery, Walthamstow.

Pioneers of the Modern Movement from William Morris to Walter Gropius by N. Pevsner (London, 1936; re-issued as *Pioneers of Modern Design*, Penguin Books, Harmondsworth, 1960).

William Morris, Medievalist and Revolutionary by M. R. Grennan (New York, 1945).

A considerable number of societies trace their origin to William Morris or look upon him as their chief founder, such as the Society for the Protection of Ancient Buildings (the famous "Antiscrape"); or the Society of Designer Craftsmen (formerly the Arts and Crafts Exhibition Society); or the Art Workers' Guild. But each of these stemmed from only one aspect of his many-sided genius. The William Morris Society, now over ten years old, seeks to cover all aspects. The society was founded in 1953 at a meeting in Red House, built for Morris in 1860 by his friend Philip Webb who is now given a high place in the long line of British architects and who for some years was treasurer of the Socialist League. The officers then chosen were Graeme Shankland as Honorary Secretary and Freeman Bass as Honorary Treasurer. The public existence of the society dates from 13th September, 1955, with a letter announcing its formation signed by J. Brandon Jones, Nikolaus Pevsner and Stanley Morison (who had been chairman of the meeting two years earlier at Red House). Sir Sydney Cockerell was president until his death in 1962, when he was succeeded by Stanley Morison. Vice-presidents have been G. D. H. Cole and, at present, Sir Basil Blackwell. The Honorary Secretary is: R. C. H. Briggs of 260 Sandycombe Road, Kew, Surrey. Amongst the transactions of the Society in the last seven years are:

Bernard Shaw and William Morris by R. Page Arnot. 1957.
The Mediæval Vision of William Morris by R. Furneaux Jordan. 1960.
William Morris as a Socialist by G. D. H. Cole. 1960.
William Morris, Writer by Jack Lindsay. 1961.
A Handlist of the Published Addresses of William Morris by R. C. H. Briggs. 1960.
William Morris and Old Norse Literature by J. N. Swannell. 1963.

Lastly there is the Kelmscott Fellowship founded early in 1919 by May Morris and a number of others such as Emery Walker, Sydney Cockerell, J. W. Mackail, J. L. Mahon, Robert Steele, Catterson-Smith etc., who had known William Morris or were partisans of his work and standpoint. May Morris (1862–1938) continued as president till her death and

127

was succeeded by Miss Dorothy Walker, daughter of Sir Emery Walker, who was a member of the Socialist League and for a time Secretary of the Hammersmith Socialist Society and a very close friend of Morris. Miss Walker continued her presidency till her own death on 20th September, 1963, at the age of eighty-five. The Fellowship continues to organise lectures and visits, of which a seventieth programme was recently sent out, and issues occasional bulletins. Its secretaries are:

H. J. Watson, 47 Rutland Gardens, Hove 3, Sussex.
A. Halcrow Verstage, 31 Horniman Drive, London, S.E.23.

INDEX

130